28 DAYS LATER

28 DAYS LATER
Alex Garland

faber and faber

First published in 2002
by Faber and Faber Ltd
The Bindery, 51 Hatton Garden
London EC1N 8HN

First published in the USA in 2002

Typeset by Country Setting, Kingsdown, Kent CT14 8ES
Printed in England by CPI Group (UK) Ltd, Croydon, CR0 4YY

A CIP record for this book is available from the British Library

ISBN 978-0-571-21653-6

2 4 6 8 10 9 7 5 3 1

CONTENTS

INTRODUCTION

28 Days Later is an original screenplay, in that it wasn't adapted from a book. But it references and is influenced by other stories to such an extent that the word 'original' feels slightly dishonest.

Our male protagonist, waking up in hospital to find an entirely new landscape outside, will be familiar to anyone who has read *Day of the Triffids*. The scene in which our heroes loot a supermarket is a set piece of post-apocalyptic wish-fulfilment, probably most brilliantly achieved by the empty mall of *Dawn of the Dead*. Mailer, the chained 'infected', is in some ways a refugee from *Day of the Dead*.

Some of these references to earlier films or books were made unconsciously. That is to say, they were written into the script, and only later would I realise that the idea had been sourced or lifted from somewhere else. However, many references were entirely deliberate. The name of the lead character, Jim, is a very respectful nod towards my hero, J. G. Ballard, whose concept-driven science-fiction novels were a constant ambient presence throughout the writing of the script. And Selena's race – specified as black rather than just happening to be black – is a kind of reference to George Romero's Night-Dawn-Day trilogy, which was notable for the black leading characters. Similarly, *Assault on Precinct 13* and *The Omega Man*. It was a convention I liked for nostalgic rather than politically correct reasons.

Other influences I should mention would certainly include David Cronenberg, Steven King, Capcom's *Resident Evil* video game series and, more obscurely, the comic strip writer/artist Daniel Clowes

If there is something misleading about the title 'original screenplay', there is something equally misleading about the writer's credit. I come from a background of novel writing; so I know what it is to write something alone – and I didn't write this screenplay alone.

The first draft of *28 Days Later* was completed towards the end of the summer of 2000. Andrew Macdonald, the film's producer, got involved from the second draft. Danny Boyle, the film's director, got involved from the fifth draft. There were almost fifty separate drafts before we reached the shooting script, and after that I lost count, but rewrites continued through filming, editing, pick-ups, re-shoots and ADR.

Throughout, Danny, Andrew and I worked together extremely closely. The screenplay, and for that matter the film as a whole, is the product of collaboration – largely between three people, although several others were centrally involved. In the case of the writer's credit, I personally see it as a term of convenience, or a rough allocation of responsibility, rather than something to be taken literally.

In respect of the collaboration, and despite the many influences in the script, I think we made a film that is primarily defined by itself. But that tends to be the way with stories. In either the telling or re-telling, the ice-flow structure is always cracking and shifting under your feet, whether you want it to or not.

Alex Garland

CAST AND CREW

Fox Searchlight and DNA Films Presents

MAIN CAST

JIM	Cillian Murphy
SELENA	Naomie Harris
HANNAH	Megan Burns
FRANK	Brendan Gleeson
PRIVATE JONES	Leo Bill
PRIVATE MITCHELL	Ricci Harnett
HENRY	Christopher Eccleston
SERGEANT FARRELL	Stuart McQuarrie
MARK	Noah Huntley
ACTIVIST	Jukka Hiltunen
ACTIVIST	Alex Palmer
FEMALE ACTIVIST	Bindu de Stoppani
MAILER	Marvin Campbell
JIM'S FATHER	Christopher Dunne
JIM'S MOTHER	Emma Hitching
SCIENTIST	David Schneider
INFECTED KID	Justin Hackney
INFECTED PRIEST	Toby Sedgwick
MR BRIDGES	Alexander Delamere
DAVIS	Sanjay Ramburuth
BEDFORD	Ray Panthaki
BELL	Junior Laniyan
CLIFTON	Luke Mably

MAIN CREW

Director	Danny Boyle
Producer	Andrew Macdonald
Writer	Alex Garland
Director of Photography	Anthony Dod Mantle
Editor	Chris Gill
Production Designer	Mark Tildesley
Art Director	Mark Digby
Line Producer	Robert How

Costume Designer	Rachael Fleming
Music	John Murphy
Sound	Glenn Freemantle
Casting	Gail Stevens
Producer's Assistant	Carey Berlin

28 Days Later

INT. MONITOR SCREEN. NIGHT.

Images of stunning violence. Looped.

Soldiers in a foreign war shoot an unarmed civilian at point-blank range; a man is set on by a frenzied crowd wielding clubs and machetes; a woman is necklaced while her killers cheer and howl.

Pull back to reveal that we are seeing one of many screens in a bank of monitors, all showing similar images . . .

Then revealing that the monitors are in a . . .

INT. SURGICAL CHAMBER. NIGHT.

. . . surgical chamber. And watching the screens is a . . .

. . . chimp, strapped to an operating table, with its skull dissected open, webbed in wires and monitoring devices, muzzled with a transparent guard. Alive.

Behind the surgical chamber, through the wide doorframe, we can see a larger laboratory beyond.

INT. BRIGHT CORRIDOR. NIGHT.

A group of black-clad ALF Activists, all wearing balaclavas, move down a corridor. They carry various gear – bag, bolt cutters.

As they move, one Activist reaches up to a security camera and sprays it black with an aerosol paint can.

INT. LABORATORY. NIGHT.

The Activists enter the laboratory.

> CHIEF ACTIVIST
> Fucking hell . . .

The Chief Activist takes his camera off his shoulder and starts taking photos.

The room is huge and long, and darkened except for specific pools of lights. Partially illuminated are rows of cages with clear perspex doors. They run down either side of the room. In the cages are chimpanzees.

Most are in a state of rabid agitation, banging and clawing against the perspex, baring their teeth through foam-flecked mouths.

They reach the far end of the lab, where on a huge steel operating table they see the dissected chimp.

FEMALE ACTIVIST

Oh God . . .

The dissected chimp's eyes flick to the Activists. Blood wells from around the exposed brain tissue.

Tears starts to roll down the Female Activist's cheeks.

CHIEF ACTIVIST
(*to Female Activist*)

Keep your shit together. If we're going to get them out of here . . .

The Finnish Activist is checking the perspex cages.

FINNISH ACTIVIST

I can pop these, no problem.

CHIEF ACTIVIST

So get to it.

The Finnish Activist raises his crowbar and sticks it around the edge of one of the doors – about to prise it open.

At that moment, the doors to the laboratory bang open.

The Activists all turn. Standing at the entrance is the Scientist.

A pause. The Scientist jumps to a telephone handset on the wall and shouts into the receiver.

SCIENTIST

Security! We have a break-in! Get to sector . . .

A hand slams down the disconnect button.

. . . nine.

The Chief Activist plucks the receiver from the Scientist's hands, and then rips the telephone from the wall.

A beat.

I know who you are, I know what you think you're doing, but you have to listen to me. You can't release these animals.

CHIEF ACTIVIST

If you don't want to get hurt, shut your mouth, and don't move a fucking muscle.

SCIENTIST
(blurts)

The chimps are infected!

The Activists hesitate, exchanging a glance.

SCIENTIST
(continuing: stumbling, flustered)

These animals are highly contagious. They've been given an inhibitor.

CHIEF ACTIVIST

Infected with what?

SCIENTIST

Chemically restricted, locked down to a . . . a single impulse that . . .

CHIEF ACTIVIST

Infected with *what*?

The Scientist hesitates before answering.

SCIENTIST

Rage

Behind the Activists, the bank of monitors show the faces of the machete-wielding crowd.

SCIENTIST
(*desperately trying to explain*)
In order to cure, you must first understand. Just imagine:
to have power over all the things we feel we can't control.
Anger, violence . . .

FINNISH ACTIVIST
What the fuck is he talking about?

CHIEF ACTIVIST
We don't have time for this shit! Get the cages open!

SCIENTIST
No!

CHIEF ACTIVIST
We're going, you sick bastard, and we're taking your torture
victims with us.

SCIENTIST
NO! You must listen! The animals are contagious! The
infection is in their blood and saliva! One bite and . . .

FEMALE ACTIVIST
They won't bite me.

*The Female Activist crouches down to face the wild eyes of the infected
chimp behind the perspex.*

SCIENTIST
STOP! You have no idea!

*The Scientist makes a desperate lunge towards her, but the Chief Activist
grabs him.*

FEMALE ACTIVIST
Good boy. You don't want to bite me, do you?

*The Female Activist gives a final benign smile, then the Finnish
Activist pops open the door.*

SCIENTIST
NO!

Like a bullet from a gun, the infected chimp leaps out at the Female Activist – and sinks its teeth into her neck. She reels back as the chimp claws and bites with extraordinary viciousness.

At the same moment, a deafening alarm begins to sound.

> FEMALE ACTIVIST
> (*shrieking*)
> Get it off! Get it off!

The Finnish Activist rips the ape off and throws it on to the floor. The infected chimp immediately bites into the man's leg. He yells with pain, and tries to kick it off.

Behind him, the Female Activist has started to scream. She doubles up, clutching the side of her head.

> I'm burning! Jesus! Help me!

> SCIENTIST
> We have to kill her!

> FEMALE ACTIVIST
> I'm burning! I'm burning!

> CHIEF ACTIVIST
> What's . . .

> SCIENTIST
> We have to kill her NOW!

Meanwhile, the Female Activist's cries have become an unwavering howl of pain – and she is joined by the Finnish Activist, whose hands have also flown to the side of his head, gripping his temples as if trying to keep his skull from exploding.

> CHIEF ACTIVIST
> What's wrong with them?

The Scientist grabs a desk-lamp base and starts running towards the screaming Female Activist . . .

. . . who has ripped off her balaclava – revealing her face – the face of an Infected.

She turns to the Scientist.

Oh God.

She leaps at him. He screams as they go tumbling to the ground.

The Chief Activist watches in immobile horror as she attacks the Scientist with amazing ferocity.

INT. CORRIDOR. NIGHT.

Another Activist makes his way down the corridor towards the lab.

ACTIVIST
(*hisses*)

Terry? Jemma?

No answer.

Mika? Where are you?

He reaches the door to the lab, which is closed – and . . .

. . . as he opens it, we realise the door is also soundproofed.

A wall of screaming hits him.

He stands in the doorway – stunned by the noise, and then the sight.

Blood, death, and his colleagues, all Infected.

ACTIVIST
(*continuing*)

Bloody hell.

The Infected rush him.

Fade to black.

Title:

28 DAYS LATER

INT. HOSPITAL ROOM. LATE AFTERNOON.

Close up of Jim, a young man in his twenties, wearing pale green hospital pyjamas. He has a month's beard, is dishevelled, and asleep.

8

We pull back to see that Jim is lying on a hospital bed, in a private room. Connected to his arms are multiple drips, a full row of four or five on each side of the bed. Most of the bags are empty.

Jim's eyes open.

He looks around with an expression of confusion. Then he sits up. He is weak, but he swings his legs off the bed and stands. The attached drips are pulled with him and clatter to the floor.

Jim winces, and pulls the taped needles from his arm.

                              JIM
    Ow . . .

His voice is hoarse, his mouth dry. Massaging his throat, he walks to the door.

INT. COMA WARD. LATE AFTERNOON.

The door to Jim's hospital room is locked. The key is on the floor. He picks it up and opens the door.

Jim exits into a corridor.

At the far end, a sign reads: COMA WARD. *There is no sign of life or movement.*

Jim walks down the corridor. One of the doors is half-open. From inside, there is the sound of buzzing flies.

INT. HOSPITAL WARDS. LATE AFTERNOON.

Jim moves as quickly as he can through the hospital, still weak, but now driven by adrenaline.

All the wards and corridors are deserted. Medical notes and equipment lie strewn over the floors, trolleys are upended, glass partition doors are smashed. In a couple of places, splashes of dried blood arc up the walls.

He reaches A&E. On one wall is a row of public payphones.

He lifts a receiver, and the line is dead. He goes down the line, trying them all.

In the corner of the A&E reception is a smashed soft-drinks machine, with a few cans collected at the base.

Jim grabs one, rips off the ring-pull and downs it in one go. Then he grabs another, and heads for the main doors.

EXT. HOSPITAL. LATE AFTERNOON.

Jim exits and walks out into the bright daylight of the forecourt. The camera begins to pull away from him.

JIM

Hello?

Aside from a quiet rush of wind, there is silence. No traffic, no engines, no movement. Not even birdsong.

EXT. LONDON. SUNDOWN.

Jim walks through the empty city, from St Thomas's Hospital, over Westminster Bridge, past the Houses of Parliament, down Whitehall, to Trafalgar Square.

A bright overhead sun bleaches the streets. A light breeze drifts litter and refuse. Cars lie abandoned, shops looted.

Jim is still wearing his hospital pyjamas, and carries a plastic bag full of soft-drink cans.

EXT. CENTRAL LONDON ROAD/CHURCH. NIGHT.

Jim walks. Night has fallen. He needs to find a place to rest . . .

He pauses. Down a narrow side street is a church. He walks towards it. The front doors are open.

INT. CHURCH. NIGHT.

Jim walks inside, moving with the respectful quietness that people adopt when entering a church.

The doors ahead to the main chamber are closed. Pushing them, gently trying the handle, it is obvious they are locked. But another open door is to his left. He goes through it.

INT. CHURCH — STAIRWELL. NIGHT.

Jim moves up a stairwell.

Writ large on the wall is a single line of graffiti: REPENT. THE END IS EXTREMELY FUCKING NIGH

INT. CHURCH — GALLERY LEVEL. NIGHT.

Jim moves into the gallery level, and sees, through the dust and rot, ornate but faded splendour. At the far end, a stained-glass window is illuminated by the moonlight.

Jim pads in, stands at the gallery, facing the stained-glass window for a moment before looking down . . .

Beneath are hundreds of dead bodies. Layered over the floor, jammed into the pews, spilling over the altar. The scene of an unimaginable massacre.

Jim stands, stunned. Then sees, standing motionless at different positions, facing away from him, four people.

Their postures and stillness make their status unclear. Jim hesitates before speaking.

JIM

. . . Hello?

Immediately, the four heads flick round. Infected.

And the next moment, there is the powerful thump of a door at the far end of the gallery.

Jim whirls to the source as the Infected below start to move.

The door thumps again – another stunningly powerful blow, the noise echoing around the chamber.

Confused, fist closing around his bag of soft drinks, Jim steps onto the gallery, facing the door . . .

. . . and it smashes open.

Revealing an Infected Priest – who locks sight on Jim, and starts to sprint.

JIM
(continuing)

Father?

The Priest is half way across the gallery.

Father, what are you . . .

And now the moonlight catches the Priest's face. Showing clearly: the eyes. The blood smeared and collected around his nose, ears and mouth. Darkened and crusted, accumulated over days and weeks. Fresh blood glistening.

Jesus!

In a movement of pure instinct, Jim swings the bag just as the Priest is about to reach him – and connects squarely with the man's head.

Oh, that was bad, that was bad . . . I shouldn't have done that . . .

He breaks into a run . . .

INT. CHURCH — STAIRWELL. NIGHT.

Down the stairwell . . .

INT. CHURCH. NIGHT.

. . . into the front entrance, where the locked door now strains under the blows of the Infected inside.

JIM

   Shit.

EXT. CHURCH. NIGHT.

Jim sprints down the stone steps.

As he reaches the bottom the doors are broken open, and the Infected give chase.

EXT. CENTRAL LONDON ROAD. NIGHT.

Jim runs – the Infected have almost reached him.

A hand fires up a Zippo lighter, and lights the rag of a Molotov cocktail.

As Jim runs, something flies past his head, and the Infected closest to him explodes in a ball of flame.

Jim turns, and sees as another Molotov cocktail explodes, engulfing two in the fireball.

He whirls, now completely bewildered.

GIRL'S VOICE

  HERE!

Another Molotov cocktail explodes. The Infected stagger from the blaze, on fire.

  OVER HERE!

Jim whirls again, and sees, further down the road . . .

*. . . Selena, a black girl, also in her twenties. She wears a small
backpack, a machete is stuck into her belt – and she holds a lit
Molotov cocktail in her hand.*

. . . and Mark, a tall, good-looking man – throwing another bottle.

It smashes on the head of the last of the Infected, bathing it in flame . . .

The burning Infected bumps blindly into a car. Falls. Gets up again.

*Blindly, it staggers off the road, into a petrol station – where an
abandoned car has run over one of the pumps.*

The ground beneath it suddenly ignites, and the petrol station explodes.

EXT. SIDE STREET. NIGHT.

Selena and Mark lead Jim into a side street.

JIM
(*dazed*)
Those people! Who were . . . who . . .

MARK
This way! Move it!

Jim allows himself to be hurried along.

EXT. SHOP. NIGHT.

Selena stops outside a newsagent's shop. The shop's door and windows are covered with a metal security grill, but the grill over the door lock has been prised away enough for Selena to slip her hand through to the latch.

INT. SHOP. NIGHT.

Inside, most of the shelves have been emptied of confectionery. Newspapers and magazines litter the floor. The magazine covers of beautiful girls and sports cars have become instant anachronisms.

At the back of the shop, a makeshift bed of sheets and sleeping bag is nestled. This has obviously been Selena and Mark's home for the last few days.

INT. NEWSAGENT. NIGHT.

Jim, Mark and Selena enter the newsagent's and pull down the grill.

MARK
A man walks into a bar with a giraffe. They each get pissed. The giraffe falls over. The man goes to leave and the barman says, you can't leave that lying there. The man says, it's not a lion. It's a giraffe.

Silence.

Mark pulls off his mask and turns to Selena.

He's completely humourless. You two will get along like a house on fire.

15

Selena, who has already taken off her mask, ignores Mark.

SELENA

Who are you? You've come from a hospital.

MARK

Are you a doctor?

SELENA

He's not a doctor. He's a patient.

JIM

I'm a bicycle courier. I was riding a package from
Farringdon to Shaftesbury Avenue. A car cut across me . . .
and then I wake up in hospital, today . . . I wake up and
I'm hallucinating, or . . .

MARK

What's your name?

JIM

Jim.

MARK

I'm Mark. This is Selena. (*Beat.*) Okay, Jim. We've got some
bad news.

*Selena starts to tell her story, and as the story unfolds we see the
images she describes.*

SELENA

It began as rioting. And right from the beginning, you knew
something bad was going on because the rioters were killing
people. And then it wasn't on the TV any more. It was in
the street outside. It was coming through your windows.
We all guessed it was a virus. An infection. You didn't need
a doctor to tell you that. It was the blood. Something in
the blood. By the time they tried to evacuate the cities, it
was already too late. The infection was everywhere. The
army blockades were overrun. And that was when the
exodus started. The day before the radio and TV stopped
broadcasting there were reports of infection in Paris and
New York. We didn't hear anything more after that.

JIM

Where are your families?

MARK

They're dead.

SELENA

Yours will be dead too.

JIM

No . . . No! I'm going to find them. They live in Greenwich.
I can walk. (*Heading for the exit.*) I'm going to . . . to go
and . . .

SELENA

You'll go and come back.

JIM

(*pulling at the grill*)

Yes! I'll go and come back.

MARK

Rules of survival. Lesson one – you never go anywhere
alone, unless you've got no choice. Lesson two – you only
move during daylight, unless you've got no choice. We'll
take you tomorrow. Then we'll all go and find your dead
parents together. Okay?

EXT. TRAIN TRACKS. DAY.

*Jim, Selena and Mark walk along the Docklands Light Railway in
single file. Ahead is a train.*

*Behind the train, as if spilled in its wake, are abandoned bags,
suitcases, backpacks.*

Mark drops pace to let Jim catch up.

MARK

How's your head? Fucked?

No reply.

MARK
(*continuing, gesturing at the city*)
I know where your head is. You're looking at these
windows, these millions of wlndows, and you're thinking –
there's no way this many people are dead. It's just too many
windows.

Mark picks up a handbag from the tracks.

The person who owned this bag. Can't be dead.

*Mark reaches in and starts to pull things out as they walk, discarding
the personal possessions.*

A woman – (*car keys*) – who drove a Nissan Micra – (*teddy*) –
and had a little teddy bear – (*condoms*) – and carried
protection, just in case.

Mark tosses the condoms behind him.

MARK
(*continuing, dry*)
Believe me, we won't need them any more than she will.

He hands the bag to Jim and walks ahead.

Jim pulls out a mobile phone.

He switches it on.

It reads: SEARCHING FOR NETWORK.

The message blinks a couple of times. Then the screen goes blank.

Jim looks left.

*He is now alongside the train. The inside of the windows are smeared
with dried blood. Pressed against the glass is the face of a dead man.*

*Jim drops the phone and breaks into a run – running past Mark and
Selena.*

MARK
(*continuing, hissing*)
Hey!

EXT. GREENWICH COMMON. DAY.

Jim, Selena and Mark jog across Greenwich Common. Jim gestures towards one of the streets on the far side of the green.

> JIM
> (*low voice*)
> Down there. Westlink Street. Second on the left.

EXT. WESTLINK STREET. DAY.

The street is modest red-brick semi-detached houses. They stand outside Number 43. Jim waits while Selena scans the dark facade.

> SELENA
> If there's anyone in there who isn't human . . .

> JIM
> I understand.

> SELENA
> Anyone.

> JIM
> I understand.

Selena shoots a glance at Jim. Jim is gazing at the house.

> MARK
> Okay.

EXT. BACK GARDEN. DAY.

Jim uses the key under the flowerpot to open the back door.

INT. HOUSE. DAY.

Jim, Selena and Mark move quietly through the kitchen and the downstairs of the house. Surprisingly, everything is neat and tidy. Washed plates are stacked by the sink, newspapers on the table are neatly piled. The headline on the top paper reads simply:
CONTAINMENT FAILS.

They reach the bottom of the stairs. Selena gestures upwards, and Jim nods. They start to ascend.

At the top of the stairs, Selena sniffs the air, and recoils. Jim has noticed it too. His eyes widen in alarm.

> MARK
> (*whispers*)

Wait.

But Jim pushes past and advances along the top landing, until he reaches a door. By now the smell is so bad that he is having to cover his nose and mouth with the sleeve of one arm.

Jim pushes open the door. Inside, two decomposed bodies lie side by side on the bed, intertwined. On the bedside table are an empty bottle of sleeping pills and a bottle of red wine.

Mark appears behind him. Jim stares at his parents for a couple of moments, then Mark closes the door.

INT. BATHROOM. DAY.

Jim sits on the toilet, alone. He is crying. In his hand is a piece of paper: 'Jim – with endless love, we left you sleeping. Now we're sleeping with you. Don't wake up.'

The paper crumples in his fist.

INT. LIVING ROOM. DAY.

Jim, Selena and Mark sit in the living room, on the two sofas. Jim looks dazed, uncomprehending. Selena watches Jim, her expression neutral.

> SELENA

They died peacefully. You should be grateful.

> JIM

I'm not grateful.

Jim's words hang a moment. Then Mark talks, simply, unemotionally, matter-of-fact throughout.

MARK

The roads out were all jammed. So we went to Paddington Station. Hoping: maybe we could get to Heathrow, maybe buy our way on a plane. My dad had all this cash, even though cash was already useless, and Mum had her jewellery. But twenty thousand other people had the same idea. (*A moment.*) The crowd was surging, and I lost my grip on my sister's hand. I remember realising the ground was soft. I looked down, and I was standing on people. Like a carpet, people who had fallen, and . . . somewhere in the crowd there were infected. It spread fast, no one could run, all you could do was climb. Over more people. So I did that. I got up, somehow, on top of a kiosk. (*A moment.*) Looking down, you couldn't tell which faces were infected and which weren't. With the blood, the screaming, they all looked the same. And I saw my dad. Not my mum or my sister. But I saw my dad. His face.

A short silence.

Selena's right. You should be grateful.

SELENA

We don't have time to get back to the shop before dark. We should stay here tonight.

Jim nods. He isn't sure what he wants to say.

JIM

My old room was at the end of the landing. You two take it. I'll sleep down here.

SELENA

We'll sleep in the same room. It's safer.

EXT. LONDON. DAY TO NIGHT.

The red orb of the sun goes down; the light fades. As night falls, London vanishes into blackness, with no electric light to be seen.

Then the moon appears from behind the cloud layer, and the dark city is revealed.

INT. HOUSE. NIGHT.

Jim is on the sofa. In the moonlight, we can see that his eyes are open, wide awake. Selena is curled on the other sofa, and Mark is on the floor – both asleep. The house is silent.

Jim watches Selena sleeping for a couple of moments.

Then, quietly, he gets off the sofa and pads out of the living room, down the hall to the kitchen.

INT. KITCHEN. NIGHT.

Jim enters, standing just inside the doorway. He looks around the room. On one wall, a faded kid's drawing of a car is framed. Above the counter, on a shelf of cookery books, an album has a handwritten label on the spine: 'Mum's Favourite Recipes'.

Jim walks to the fridge. Stuck to the door is a photo of Jim with his parents, arm in arm, smiling at the camera. Jim is on his mountain bike, wearing his courier bag.

Flash cut to:

Jim, sitting at the kitchen table as his Mum enters, carrying bags of shopping. Jim walks over to the bags and pulls out a carton of orange juice, which he puts straight to his mouth and begins to gulp down.

His Dad walks in from the garden.

>   JIM'S DAD
> Give me a glass of that, would you?

>   JIM
>   *(draining the carton, and giving it a shake)*
> It's empty.

Cut back to:

Jim touches the photo, their faces, lightly.

Jim is facing away from the back door, which has a large frosted-glass panel.

Through the glass panel, unseen by Jim, a dark silhouette looms against the diffused glow from the moonlight.

Through the kitchen window, a second silhouette appears.

Then there is a scratching noise from the back door.

Jim freezes.

Slowly, he turns his head, and sees the dark shapes behind the door and window.

A beat – then the door is abruptly and powerfully smashed in. It flies open, and hangs, loosely held by the bottom hinge. Standing in the doorframe is an Infected Man.

Jim shouts with alarm as the Man lunges at him – and they both go tumbling to the floor. At the same moment, the figure behind the kitchen window smashes the glass, and an Infected Teenage Girl starts to clamber through the jagged frame.

The Man gets on top of Jim, while Jim uses his arms to hold back the ferocious assault. A single strand of saliva flies from the Man's lips, and contacts Jim's cheek.

JIM
(*screams*)

Help!

Suddenly, Selena is there, holding her machete. The blade flashes down to the back of the Man's neck. Blood gushes.

Jim rolls the Infected Man off, just in time to see . . .

. . . Mark dispatch the Girl half way through the kitchen window. The Girl is holding Mark, but her legs are caught on the broken glass.

Mark jabs upwards into the Girl's torso – she stiffens, then slumps, and as Mark steps back we see he is holding a knife.

Jim hyperventilates, staring at the corpse on the kitchen floor.

It's Mr Bridges . . .

Selena turns to Jim. She is hyperventilating too, but there is control and steel in her voice.

SELENA

Were you bitten?

JIM

He lives four doors down . . .

Jim turns to the Girl sprawled halfway through the window.

That's his daughter . . .

SELENA

Were you bitten?

Jim looks at her. Selena is still holding her machete at the ready.

JIM

No . . . No! I wasn't!

SELENA

Did any of the blood get in your mouth?

JIM

No!

SELENA

Mark?

Jim turns to Mark. He is standing in the middle of the room. Stepped away from the window. The Girl's blood is on his arm – and he is wiping it away . . .

. . . off the skin . . . where a long scratch cut wells up fresh blood.

A moment.

Then Mark looks at Selena, as if slightly startled.

MARK

Wait.

But Selena is swiping with her machete. Mark lifts his arm instinctively, defensively, and the blade sinks in.

Selena immediately yanks it back.

MARK
(continuing)

DON'T!

Selena swipes again – and the blade catches Mark hard in the side of the head. Mark falls.

Jim watches, scrabbling backwards on the floor away from them, as Selena brutally finishes Mark off.

Selena looks at Mark's body for a couple of beats, then lowers the blade. She picks up a dishcloth from the sink counter and tosses it to Jim.

> SELENA

Get that cleaned off.

Jim picks up the rag and hurriedly starts to wipe the Infected's blood from around his neck.

Do you have any clothes here?

> JIM
> *(fazed, frightened of her)*

I . . . I don't know. I think so.

> SELENA

Then get them. And get dressed. We have to leave, now.

With practised speed, Selena starts to open the kitchen cupboards, selecting packets of biscuits and cans from the shelves, and stuffing them into her backpack.

More infected will be coming. They always do.

EXT. HOUSE. NIGHT.

Jim and Selena exit the front door. Jim has changed out of his hospital gear into jeans and a sweatshirt. He also has a small backpack, and is carrying a baseball bat.

EXT. LONDON ROAD. NIGHT.

Jim and Selena walk: fast, alert. But something is not being said between them . . . until Jim breaks the silence.

> JIM
> *(quiet)*

How did you know?

Selena says nothing. Continues walking.

> JIM
> *(continuing, insistent)*

How did you know he was infected?

SELENA

The blood.

JIM

The blood was everywhere. On me, on you, and . . .

SELENA
(*cutting in*)
I didn't know he was infected. Okay? I didn't know. He
knew. I could see it in his face. (*A moment.*) You need to
understand, if someone gets infected, you've got somewhere
between ten and twenty seconds to kill them. They might
be your brother or your sister or your oldest friend. It
makes no difference. Just so as you know, if it happens to
you, I'll do it in a heart-beat.

A moment.

JIM

How long had you known him?

SELENA

Five days. Or six. Does it matter?

Jim says nothing.

He was full of plans. Long-distance weapons, so they don't
get close. A newsagent's with a metal grill, so you can sleep.
Petrol bombs, so the blood doesn't splash.

Selena looks at Jim dispassionately.

Got a plan yet, Jim? You want us to find a cure and save the
world? Or fall in love and fuck?

Selena looks away again.

Plans are pointless. Staying alive is as good as it gets.

Silence.

They walk. Jim following a few steps behind Selena.

*A few moments later, Jim lifts a hand, opens his mouth, about to say
something – but Selena cuts him off without even looking round.*

Shhh.

She has seen something . . .

A line of tower blocks some distance away, standing against the night sky. In one of them, hanging in the window of one of the highest storeys, coloured fairy lights are lit up, blinking gently.

INT. TOWER BLOCK. NIGHT.

Jim and Selena walk through the smashed glass doors of the tower block. It is extremely dark inside.

Selena switches on a flashlight and illuminates the entrance hall. It is a mess. The floor is covered in broken glass and dried blood. The lift doors are jammed open, and inside is a dense bundle of rags – perhaps an old corpse, but impossible to tell, because the interior of the lift has been torched. It is black with carbon, and smoke-scarring runs up the outside wall.

Selena moves the flashlight to the stairwell. There is a huge tangle of shopping trolleys running up the stairs.

Selena gives one of the trolleys an exploratory tug. It shifts, but holds fast, meshed in with its neighbour. Then she puts a foot into one of the grates, and lifts herself up. Shining her light over the top of the tangle, she can see a gap along the top.

> JIM
> Let's hope we don't have to get out of here in a hurry.

She begins to climb through.

INT. TOWER BLOCK. NIGHT.

Jim and Selena move steadily and quietly up the stairwell, into the building. Reaching a next landing, they check around the corner before proceeding. Through a broken window, we can see that they are already high above most London buildings, and on the wall a sign reads: LEVEL 5.

> SELENA
> Need a break?

28

JIM
(*completely out of breath*)

No. You?

SELENA

No.

They continue a few steps.

JIM

I *do* need a break, by the way.

Selena nods. They stop on the stairs. Jim slips off his backpack and sits, pulling a face as he does so . . .

SELENA

What's up?

JIM

Nothing.

She gives him a cut-the-crap expression.

I've got a headache.

SELENA

Bad?

JIM

Pretty bad.

SELENA

Why didn't you say something before?

JIM

Because I didn't think you'd give a shit.

A moment, where it's unclear how Selena will react to this. Then she slips off her own backpack.

SELENA
(*going through the bag*)

You've got no fat on you, and all you've had to eat is sugar. So you're crashing. Unfortunately, there isn't a lot we can do about that . . .

Selena starts to produce a wide selection of pills, looted from a chemist.

... except pump you full of painkillers, and give you more sugar to eat.

She holds up a bottle of codeine tablets, and passes it to Jim.

As for the sugar: Lilt or Tango?

> JIM
> (*chewing codeine*)
> ... Do you have Sprite?

> SELENA
> Actually, I did have a can of Sprite, but ...

Suddenly there is a loud scream, coming from somewhere lower down the building. Jim and Selena both make a grab for their weapons.

> JIM

Jesus!

> SELENA

Quiet.

The scream comes again. The noise is chilling, echoing up the empty stairwell.

But there is something strange about it. The noise is human, but oddly autistic. It is held for slightly too long, and stops abruptly.

That's an infected.

Then, the sound of metal scraping, clattering the blockade.

> SELENA

They're in.

INT. SHOPPING TROLLEY BLOCKADE. NIGHT.

Two Infected, a Young Asian Guy and a Young White Guy, moving with amazing speed over the blockade.

INT. STAIRS. NIGHT.

Jim and Selena sprint up the stairs. Behind them, we can hear the Infected, giving chase, howling.

They pass level eight, nine, ten . . .

Jim is exhausted.

                              SELENA
        Come *on*!

                              JIM
                (out of breath, barely able to speak)
        I can't.

Selena continues, and Jim looks over the edge of the stairwell, to the landing below . . .

. . . where the two Infected appear, tearing around the corner.

INT. STAIRWELL. NIGHT.

Selena sprints up the stairs . . . and Jim sprints past her, in an amazing burst of energy and speed.

They round another bend in the stairwell . . .

. . . then both Jim and Selena scream. Standing directly in front of them is a Man in riot cop gear – helmet with full visor, gloves, a riot shield in one hand, and a length of lead pipe in the other.

The Man lunges past both of them, barging past, where the Infected White Man has appeared at the stairwell.

The Riot Gear Man swings his lead pipe and connects viciously with the White Man's head. The White Man falls backwards against the Asian Man. Both fall back down the stairs.

The Riot Gear Man turns back to Jim and Selena.

                              MAN
        Down the corridor! Flat 157!

Jim and Selena are stunned, but start to run down the corridor.

The Asian Man is coming back up the stairs. Jim looks back over his shoulder in time to see the Man deliver a massive blow to the Asian Man's head.

INT. CORRIDOR. NIGHT.

Jim and Selena run towards Flat 157. The door is open, but as they approach, it suddenly slams shut.

> JIM AND SELENA
> ((*hammering on the door*)

Let us *in*!

> GIRL
> (*out of shot*)

Who is it?

> SELENA

Let us in!

The door opens a fraction, on the chain. The face of a girl appears. She is fourteen, pale, solemn-faced.

> GIRL

Where's Dad?

Jim looks back down the corridor.

At the far end, the Man appears. He is holding the limp body of one of the Infected – and he tips it over the balcony, where it drops down the middle of the stairwell.

> MAN
> (*calls back*)

It's okay, Hannah. Let them inside.

The door closes, we hear the chain being slipped off, then it opens again.

INT. FLAT. NIGHT.

Jim and Selena enter past the pale-faced girl. The flat is council, three-bed, sixteenth floor of the block. It has patterned wallpaper, and nice but boring furnishings. It is lit by candles.

The entrance hall leads straight to the living room, which has French windows and a small balcony outside.

On one wall, a framed photograph hangs, which shows the Man standing beside a black taxi cab. Next to him is a middle aged woman – presumably the Man's wife. Hannah sits at the cab's steering wheel, beaming.

Another photo, beside, shows Hannah sat in the seat of a go-kart.

The Man follows Jim and Selena inside.

MAN

Come in, come in.

They follow the Man through to the living room, and Hannah recloses the front door, which has an impressive arrangement of locks and dead-bolts.

INT. FLAT – LIVING ROOM. NIGHT.

In the living room, the fairy lights hang in the window, powered by a car battery. Lit by their glow, the Man goes through a careful ritual of shedding his gear, helped by Hannah.

First, he lays down the riot shield. Then he puts the bloodsmeared lead pipe on a small white towel. Next, he removes his gloves – and places them beside the bar on the towel. Then he folds the towel over the weapon and gloves, and puts it beside the riot shield. Finally he removes the visored helmet.

Jim and Selena watch him. They look pretty rattled, not really knowing what to expect.

After the Man has finished shedding his gear, he turns.

MAN

So . . . I'm Frank, anyway.

He extends his hand to Jim and Selena. Jim hesitates very briefly, then shakes it.

JIM

I'm Jim.

SELENA
Selena.

Frank beams, and suddenly he seems much less frightening and imposing. If anything, he is just as nervous as Jim and Selena.

FRANK

Jim and Selena. Good to meet you. And this is my daughter, Hannah. (*Turning to Hannah.*) . . . Come on, sweetheart. Say hello.

Hannah takes a step into the room, but says nothing.

So . . . so this is great. Just great. It calls for a celebration, I'd say. Why don't you all sit down, and . . . Hannah, what have we got to offer?

HANNAH
(*quietly*)
We've got Mum's *crème de menthe*.

An awkward beat.

FRANK

Yes, her *crème de menthe*. Great. Look, sit, please. Get comfortable. Sit tight while I get it.

Frank exits. Selena, Jim and Hannah all stand, until Selena gestures at the sofa.

SELENA
Shall we?

Jim and Selena take the sofa. Hannah stays standing.

FRANK
(*out of shot*)
Where are the bloody glasses?

HANNAH
Middle cupboard.

FRANK
(*out of shot*)
No! The good ones! This is a celebration!

HANNAH

Top cupboard.

Another short, uncomfortable pause. Hannah looks at Jim and Selena from her position near the doorway. Her expression is blank and unreadable.

JIM

This is your place, then.

Hannah nods.

It's nice.

Hannah nods again.

Frank re-enters. Frank is beaming, holding the crème de menthe, *and four wine glasses.*

FRANK

There! I know it isn't much but . . . well, cheers!

EXT. TOWER BLOCK. NIGHT.

The moon shines above the tower block.

INT. FLAT. NIGHT.

Jim, Selena and Hannah all sit in the living room, sipping the crème de menthe. *Frank is disconnecting the fairy lights as he talks, and pulling the curtains closed, rather systematically checking for cracks along the edges.*

FRANK

Normally we keep the windows covered at night, because the light attracts them. But when we saw your petrol station fire, we knew it had to be survivors . . . So we hooked up the Christmas tree lights. Like a beacon.

Finished with the sofa, he sits on the armchair.

SELENA

We're grateful.

FRANK

Well, we're grateful you came. I was starting to really worry. Like I say, we haven't seen any sign of anyone normal for a while now.

JIM

There aren't any others in the building?

Frank shakes his head.

SELENA

And you haven't seen any people outside?

Frank's eyes flick to Hannah.

FRANK

We haven't left the block for more than two weeks. Stayed right here. Only sensible thing to do. Everyone who went out . . .

SELENA

Didn't come back.

FRANK

And there's two hundred flats here. Most of them have a few cans of food, or cereal, or something.

SELENA

It's a good set-up.

FRANK

It isn't bad.

He puts a hand on Hannah's shoulder, and gives it a squeeze.

We've got by, haven't we?

INT. BATHROOM. NIGHT.

Jim is in the bathroom, inspecting himself in the mirror. He is just finishing shaving his beard off, and has had to use the razor dry. He has cut himself several times.

Jim does a couple of last dry strokes with the razor, and winces as he cuts himself again. He uses spit to wipe away the blood.

Then, from outside, Frank speaks.

> FRANK
> (*out of shot*)
> You okay in there, Jim?

> JIM
> Yes. Fine.

> FRANK
> (*out of shot*)
> Sorry we couldn't spare the water but . . . it's the same with the toilet. The, er, flush doesn't work. I'm afraid you have to use the bucket.

Jim opens the door.

> FRANK
> Have to empty it each morning. We just chuck it over the balcony . . . No mod cons here.

> JIM
> It's fine.

> FRANK
> . . . Well, look, it's pretty late. I'm going to turn in. We've got a spare room. Are you and Selena . . . ?

> JIM
> I'll take the living room.

> FRANK
> Oh, right. I mean, yes . . . So, goodnight then, anyway.

> JIM
> Goodnight, Frank.

Frank smiles, and heads to his bedroom.

INT. FLAT. NIGHT.

Jim feels his way down the dark corridor back to the candlelit living room. Selena is standing by the window. She looks around when Jim enters.

SELENA

Very spruce.

JIM

Very shredded.

SELENA

Uh-huh.

Jim sits on the armchair, and Selena moves to look at a picture on the wall – the photo of Frank's family and the black cab.

JIM

So what do you make of them?

SELENA

They're desperate. Probably need us more than we need them.

JIM

. . . I think they're good people.

SELENA

Good people?

JIM

Yeah.

SELENA

Well, that's nice. But you should be more concerned about whether they're going to slow you down.

JIM

Right. Because if they slowed you down . . .

SELENA

I'd leave them behind.

JIM

In a heart beat.

SELENA

Yeah.

JIM

I wouldn't.

SELENA

Then you're going to wind up getting yourself killed.

A moment. Then Selena stands.

I'm going to get some sleep.

JIM

Selena – you think I don't get it. But I do get it. And I know I'd be dead already if I hadn't met you.

Selena hesitates at the door – then turns.

SELENA

Sure.

JIM

No, look – I mean thank you.

SELENA

And I mean sure. Goodnight, Jim.

JIM

She exits, leaving Jim alone.

Goodnight.

Jim walks around the room, blowing out the candles. He leaves one burning beside the sofa.

Then he slides open the French doors and exits out onto the balcony.

EXT. BALCONY. NIGHT.

The city is spread out in front of Jim. In the distance, to the north, the petrol station still burns, sending billowing clouds of sparks high into the night sky.

INT. FLAT. EARLY MORNING.

Jim sits on the armchair, facing the window, nursing a can of Lilt. Outside, the sky has just started to brighten with first light.

Frank enters.

                    FRANK
Morning, Jim.

                     JIM
Morning.

                    FRANK
Listen, have you got a minute?

EXT. TOWER BLOCK ROOF. EARLY MORNING.

Frank and Jim appear from a service door. The view over London is spectacular – low clouds catching the sunrise, and a plume of smoke still drifting up from the petrol station blaze. But more noticeable is that the entire roof area is covered in buckets, pans, bowls, plates . . .

                    FRANK
We lost water pressure three weeks ago. For a while, I thought we'd be okay with the water in the other flats. The cisterns and tanks. But it vanishes so quick you wouldn't believe. You drink it, it evaporates, turns stagnant . . .

JIM
(*looking in the pans*)
They're all empty . . .

FRANK
It hasn't rained in over a week.

Frank sits, watching Jim.

You can set up a plastic sheet to catch dew and condensation.
Trap it somehow. I saw it on TV once and I've been
experimenting, but I can't get it to work, and . . . you don't
happen to . . .

Jim shakes his head.

You'd never think it. Needing rain so badly . . . Not in
fucking England . . . (*He breaks off.*) Jim, we don't have
enough water for you and Selena.

A moment.

JIM
Right.

FRANK
No. It's not what you think.

INT. FLAT. DAY.

*Jim, Selena, Frank and Hannah all sit in the living room. Frank is
on the armchair. On the coffee table in front of him is a small radio.
He turns it on – producing a fuzz of radio static.*

SELENA
There haven't been any broadcasts for weeks.

FRANK
(*interrupting*)
Just listen.

*They listen. Through the static, the sound of a voice begins to sift
through.*

VOICE

The answer to infection is here . . . if you can hear this, you're not alone . . . there are others like you . . . other survivors... we are soldiers, we are armed and we can protect you . . .

The Voice fades into the static.

SELENA
(*amazed*)

Soldiers.

FRANK

There's more. Listen.

VOICE

Our location is the forty-second blockade, the M602, twenty-seven miles north-east of Manchester . . . you must find us . . .

FRANK

Then it just repeats.

JIM

It's a recording?

Frank switches the radio off, and produces a map of Britain, which he opens on the table.

FRANK

It's a recording. But this is where it's telling us to go.

Frank points to the location described.

JIM

The North . . .

FRANK

The way things are, we might need two or three days to get up there.

SELENA

We.

A moment. Then Frank gives a short, embarrassed laugh.

FRANK

Sound carries in this flat. Jerry-built, I suppose, and . . . me
and Hannah do need you more than you need us.

SELENA

I wasn't —

FRANK

It's okay. Look, it's the truth. I can't leave the block if it's
just the two of us. If something happened to me, Hannah
would be alone. But if we were with other people . . .

*He lets the sentence hang, gazing at Jim and Selena with undisguised
hope.*

SELENA

If it's a recording, for all we know the soldiers who made it
are dead.

FRANK

Yes. It's possible.

SELENA

And that stuff about the answer to infection. There is no
answer to infection. It's already done pretty much all the
damage it can.

JIM

Maybe they've got a cure.

SELENA

Maybe they've got nothing at all.

FRANK

The only way to find out is to reach them.

SELENA

We could die trying.

HANNAH

Or die here.

Hannah speaks so rarely that her interjection seems to take everyone by surprise. Including her. For a moment she looks flustered, but then she continues.

> And anyway, it isn't true what Dad said. You need us just the same as we need you. We need each other. And we'll never be safe in the cities, and soldiers could keep us safe.

She pauses for a breath.

> So we have to try and get there.

A beat.

JIM

> Get there how?

Cut to:

EXT. TOWER BLOCK. DAY.

A black London cab drives fast out of the tower block's underground garage, bursting into the daylight.

INT. CAB. DAY.

Hannah and Selena sit on the back seat, and Jim sits on the fold-down. Frank smiles, starts the meter running, and leans around to his passengers.

FRANK

> Just so as you know. I don't take cheques or credit cards.

EXT. CAB. DAY.

Frank drives through the destroyed streets of the capital.

They pass a stray Infected, through the smashed window of a shop. Its head flicks around at the noise of the cab's engine, and starts to move, but the cab is moving too fast to catch.

EXT. CAB/TUNNEL ENTRANCE — SOUTH. DAY.

The cab pulls up at the entrance of a tunnel that leads under the river Thames.

FRANK

What do you think?

SELENA

It's the most direct route to the other side of the river.

JIM

Then we should go the indirect route. The one in broad
daylight. That isn't underground.

FRANK

Let's just get it done.

Frank floors the accelerator and they head into the tunnel.

INT. CAB. DAY.

*Frank drives through the tunnel. Wrecked cars and debris are
illuminated in the headlights, and Frank weaves expertly between
them. His passengers roll with the movement of the cab.*

JIM

I knew this was a shit idea. You know why? Because it was
really obviously a shit idea. Driving into a dark tunnel, full
of smashed cars and broken glass *is really fucking obviously
a shit idea.*

*As Jim speaks, out of the gloom, caught in the headlights, a huge pile
of cars appears, stretching across the full width of the tunnel.*

Frank slams his foot down on the accelerator.

JIM
(*continuing*)

Oh no.

EXT. CAB. DAY.

The cab bumps up onto the barricade and drives over.

INT. CAB. DAY.

*The cab bumps down the other side of the barricade, with a cheer from
the passengers – but the jubilation only lasts a moment, because the*

45

cab hits the road hard, on to a carpet of broken glass, and the front left tyre blows.

> FRANK
> HOLD ON!

Frank saws at the wheel, but loses control. The cab scrapes along the side of an abandoned car, then slews to a halt.

Frank tries accelerating again, but the cab immediately pulls left, back into the car.

> Fuck.

Frank jumps out of the cab, and shines his flashlight around the tunnel.

> JIM
> The world's worst place to get a flat.

> FRANK
> Agreed. I think we'd better do this quick.

INT. TUNNEL. DAY.

Frank opens the boot and puts the jack into Hannah's hand.

> FRANK
> You know what to do.

Hannah immediately runs to the front of the cab and hunches down. Meanwhile, Frank unclips the spare and hauls it out.

Jim and Selena stand at the back of the cab, weapons ready, shining their flashlights into the darkness.

At the front of the cab, Hannah pumps the jack, but it is moving with aching slowness.

At the back of the cab, Jim and Selena wait nervously.

There is a noise from further down the tunnel, in the direction from which they came. A scrabbling rush of movement – but too quiet to be humans.

Jim and Selena exchange a glance.

JIM

. . . You heard that?

FRANK
(*from the front of the cab*)

Heard what?

Jim is about to answer. Then his eyes widen. He looks down . . .

JIM

Holy shit.

A tide of rats is rushing under their feet.

FRANK
(*as the rats rush around them*)

What the fuck?

SELENA

They're running from infected.

As if in answer, the howls of the Infected echo down the tunnel.

Hannah desperately positions the jack underneath the cab, as the rats run over her face.

>   FRANK
>   Hannah, get out, get out! (*to Jim and Selena*) Just lift it!
>   LIFT IT!

Jim, Selena and Frank get their hands under the side of the cab, and pull upwards. The cab rises.

Hannah, with great skill and speed, fits the new tyre, like a pit-stop mechanic at a grand prix.

>   SELENA
>   (*straining with the weight*)
>   Come on!

>   HANNAH
>   Almost there!

As Hannah puts an expert twist on the last wheel nut, the cab's back lights pick up the faces of the Infected spilling over the barricade.

>   FRANK
>   (*shouting*)
>   Go! Go!

They lunge back into the cab, just as the nearest Infected slams against the back window.

As the cab races off, Jim leans out the window.

>   JIM
>   (*at the Infected*)
>   Fuck you!

Frank jams his foot down, and they tear off.

EXT. TUNNEL EXIT – NORTH. DAY.

The cab races out.

>   FRANK
>   Honey, you're a cab driver's daughter.

EXT. CAB. DAY.

The cab drives through London, the meter steadily clocking upwards. Driving, Frank's eyes flick down to the fuel gauge. It is under a quarter full.

Green shoots are pushing through the cracks in the pavements and road, as nature begins to reclaim the city.

INT. CAB. DAY.

A high street. Suddenly Selena cranes around, seeing something.

> SELENA
> Whoa! Stop the cab! Stop the cab!

EXT. CAB. DAY.

They have stopped outside a supermarket. The windows are dark, but unbroken, and it looks as if there is still food on the shelves.

> SELENA
> Un. Believable.

She opens the door to the cab, holding her machete.

> JIM
> You're getting out?

> SELENA
> This place hasn't been looted. It's a gold mine.

> HANNAH
> But we don't know what's in there.

> SELENA
> Food and drink is what's in there. And we need it.

Selena gets out.

> JIM
> Wait!

> SELENA
> I've been living off Mars Bars and Coke for two weeks.
> I need some tinned fruit.

EXT. STREET. DAY.

Selena tries the door of the supermarket. It swings open.

INT. SUPERMARKET. DAY.

They enter silently. All carry their weapons at the ready.

They peer down the aisles. The supermarket is empty.

> SELENA
> Let's shop.

INT. SUPERMARKET. DAY.

Jim, Selena, Frank, and Hannah all split off with shopping trolleys. They look like kids in a toy store.

Cut to: Selena taking cans off the shelves, three at a time, going down the aisle.

> SELENA
> I'll have you, you, you. you . . .

Cut to: Jim taking more stuff off shelves.

Selena appears at the top of the aisle.

> Don't take anything we need to cook.

Jim looks at the item in his hand. It is caviar.

> JIM
> It's okay. I think you can eat this stuff raw.

Cut to: Frank, standing by the fruit and vegetable section, in front of a bank of rotting apples – marked ORGANIC. *Beside is a pile of apples that look fine.*

> FRANK
> Mmm. Irradiated.

Cut to: Selena finding Hannah by a huge array of chocolates.

> SELENA
> Ugh. If I never see chocolate again, it'll be too soon.

A beat, as something catches her eye. She whips it off the shelf.

Not counting Terry's Chocolate Orange, of course.

> HANNAH
> *(taking a handful of Yorkie bars)*
> Or Yorkies.

> SELENA
> Or Yorkies, obviously.

Cut to: Jim by the drinks counter, examining the label on a bottle of whisky, as Frank appears behind him.

> FRANK
> Put that back. We can't just take any crap.

> JIM
> It isn't any crap. It's whisky. It might be good to have.

> FRANK
> Who's arguing about whisky? I'm saying, don't get a cheap blend.

Frank takes a bottle of Lagavulin.

Single malt. Eighteen-year-old. Dark, full flavour.

Jim starts to back his trolley away.

Warm, but not aggressive. Peaty after-taste.

Cut to: Jim, Selena, Frank and Hannah shopping, pushing their full trolleys past the empty check-out desks. As Frank passes the till, he slaps down a credit card, and they walk off.

EXT. STREET. DAY.

The fully loaded cab drives away from the supermarket, riding low on the suspension.

INT. CAB. DAY.

The cab reaches the on-ramp to the Westway, and stops.

SELENA
We could have a problem here.

EXT. WESTWAY. DAY.

The cab sits at the back of an apparent traffic jam leading onto the Westway.

Both sides of the dual carriageway are jam-packed with abandoned cars, a deserted gridlock. All cars point in the same direction – out of town. Some of the cars are crashed, riding up on each other, rolled over, burned out.

As the camera rises upwards, we can see that the gridlock snakes along the entire distance of the flyover. Like the destroyed vehicles on the road to Basra, it stretches for miles . . .

INT. CAB. DAY.

JIM
Jesus Christ. We're never going to be able to get out of London.

FRANK
Don't you worry about that. I've sat twenty years in this seat. I've got my routes.

Cut to:

EXT. CAB. DAY.

Montage of the cab sweeping through suburban London, cutting down side streets, ducking down alleys, sometimes passing under the Westway flyover.

During the montage, we see scenes of devastation.

Jim gazes out of the window as the cab passes a huge cluster of rotting corpses, collected under and in the scoop of an abandoned bulldozer. The dead operator of the bulldozer lies a few feet away from his cabin.

The montage ends on: the cab bumping down a steep grass verge onto the motorway.

Nice cut-through.

EXT. MOTORWAY. DAY.

The cab drives down the motorway. There are still vehicles scattered, crashed, but fewer and fewer as distance is gained on the city.

INT. CAB DASHBOARD. DAY.

The needle on the fuel gauge drifts down to the red.

INT. CAB. DAY.

A truck lay-by approaches, with a shabby shack-style café.

A sign outside the café reads: CHEESEBURGERS'R'US. *And beneath:* LAST CHEESEBURGERS FOR SIXTY MILES.

In the forecourt are a couple of vehicles. A people-carrier family car, and a truck, slewed off the road.

Frank slows the cab to a halt, some hundred metres away.

FRANK
Okay. We either do this now, or we're walking.

EXT. CAB. DAY.

Everyone exits the cab. Selena takes a jerry can and a length of plastic tube from the boot, and Frank gives the ignition keys to Hannah.

FRANK
If anything goes wrong, you just drive. You put your foot down. And go as far as you can.

No response from Hannah.

You hear me, Hannah?

HANNAH
Yes, Dad.

Frank, Jim and Selena begin to walk towards the service station, holding their weapons at the ready.

EXT. LAY-BY. DAY.

Cautiously, Frank, Jim and Selena approach the truck. There is no sign of life around.

> SELENA

Stay close, Jim.

> JIM

. . . What?

> SELENA

You heard.

EXT. TRUCK. DAY.

While Jim and Selena stand guard, Frank works quickly. He prises the fuel cap off, inserts the tube, sucks into the tube, and spits as the diesel begins to flow into the jerry can.

INT. CAB. DAY.

Hannah watches from the driver's seat. She has her hands on the wheel, and is sliding her hands over the plastic, making a series of imaginary turns, shifting gears . . .

EXT. TRUCK. DAY.

As they wait for the can to fill, Jim tosses his bat into the air, giving it a single flip, catching it as the handle comes back round . . . being a bit flash.

Selena notices, and does not look impressed.

Almost in response to her nonplussed gaze, Jim begins to walk towards the café.

> SELENA

Where are you going?

Jim points his bat in the direction of the café.

We've got enough food.

JIM

We don't have any cheeseburgers. (*to himself*) 'Stay close.'
It's like going on holiday with your fucking aunt.

INT. CAFE. DAY.

*Jim walks inside the cafe, and finds the aftermath of carnage.
Decomposed bodies lie scattered, on and under tables: a couple of men,
a female cook, and a young family.*

Jim walks towards the family.

*The father sits wedged between the seats and the table, which are both
bolted to the floor. His neck is snapped, head hanging backwards.*

*The mother lies a couple of feet away, on the floor, half over an infant,
as if in a final protective gesture.*

Jim looks down at them.

Then there is a noise behind.

*Instinctively Jim snaps around, swinging the bat as he does so – and
connects against a small body, which flies backwards.*

*Only then do we – and Jim – see what he has hit. Crumpled,
motionless on the ground is an Infected Kid, an eight-year-old boy.*

A moment. Jim looks stunned, appalled.

Then the Infected Kid's eyes flick open. Still alive.

Jim's baseball bat swings down.

EXT. TRUCK. DAY.

The can is full. Frank removes the tube.

Jim appears.

SELENA

Find anything?

Jim says nothing.

Find anything, Jim?

> JIM

No.

Selena lets it pass – and the moment is broken as Frank stands with the can.

> FRANK

Okay. We're done.

He lifts a hand to Hannah.

INT. CAB. DAY.

Hannah smiles, turns the ignition, and throws the cab into gear.

EXT. FORECOURT. DAY.

The cab tears towards Jim, Selena and Frank, then – at the last moment – flips into a handbrake turn, and drifts to a neat stop, a couple of metres from them.

> HANNAH
> (*leaning out of the window*)

I am a cab driver's daughter.

> FRANK

You're Ayrton Senna's bloody daughter.

INT. CAB. DAY.

The cab drives down the motorway, fuel needle pressed up against the full mark. The meter runs up a tab of over three hundred pounds . . .

EXT. CAB. DAY.

They pass a sign for MANCHESTER – 130 MILES.

INT. CAB. DAY.

The occupants have settled into the reflective silence of a long drive.

Selena seems lost in thought. She looks at Jim, who has his hand stuck out the window, and is using his hand like an aerofoil, catching the wind, dipping and rising.

Then she looks at Frank, and notices . . .

. . . Frank glance in the rear-view mirror at Hannah, who catches her dad's eye. Frank smiles, and gives her a wink.

EXT. CAB. DAY.

The cab drives along A-roads.

INT. CAB. LATE AFTERNOON.

Jim is looking through some of the bags of food.

> JIM
> Who's unbelievably hungry?

> ALL
> Me.

Jim looks out of the window. They are in completely empty, rolling countryside, stretching for miles.

> JIM
> Let's have a picnic.

EXT. PICNIC SPOT. LATE AFTERNOON.

They have stopped in a beautiful spot, quite high, clear view. It is a beautiful day. The late-afternoon sunshine is bright over the green fields, trees cast long shadows.

Everyone is happily sat on the grass, eating from their hoard.

Jim has pulled open a packet of stale hot-cross buns; Hannah empties a packet of Maltesers into her mouth; Frank holds a block of cheddar, taking bites from the cheese as if it were cake; Selena drinks from a can of tinned peaches, swallowing the pieces almost whole, with the juice running down her chin.

SELENA

Oh my God, yes. I can taste the vitamin C. I can feel it in my blood.

JIM
(*cracking a bun in half*)
These are great. They're like huge biscuits.

He offers half to Hannah, who takes a bite.

HANNAH
It's true. They are like biscuits.

JIM
(*completely unintelligible, mouth full, spraying crumbs*)
An de phraisins ar phrill moipht.

Hannah and Selena laugh.

HANNAH
(*to Jim*)

What did you say?

JIM
(*swallowing*)
I said, the raisins are still moist.

Selena and Hannah laugh again.

FRANK

Hey.

Everyone turns.

Look over there.

Some distance away, in the fields below, a group of three horses – two adults and a foal – are galloping over the fields as if wild. A majestic and surreal sight, and it somehow implies the way the world will change.

HANNAH
Do you think they're infected?

FRANK
No. I think they're doing just fine.

EXT. FIELDS. LATE AFTERNOON.

The horses gallop, leaping a stone wall, and away.

EXT. PICNIC SPOT. SUNSET.

The meal has been eaten. Frank sits, playing with his radio, trying to listen to the faint broadcast. Beside him, Hannah lies on her back, eyes closed.

EXT. FENCE GATE. SUNSET.

Jim and Selena have walked a little distance away from the others, and are sat on a fence gate, looking over the view.

JIM

You know what I was thinking?

Selena considers this a moment.

SELENA

You were thinking that you'll never hear another piece of original music ever again. You'll never read a book that isn't already written. Or see a film that isn't already shot.

Jim smiles.

JIM

That's what you were thinking.

SELENA

No . . . I was thinking I was wrong.

JIM

About what?

Selena doesn't reply for a moment. Then she turns to look at Frank and Hannah – who look oddly normal, surrounded by the food wrappers from the picnic, Frank listening to the radio.

SELENA

All the death, all the shit – it doesn't really mean anything for Frank and Hannah. Because she's got her dad, and he's got his daughter, so . . . it's okay.

A beat.

SELENA
(*continuing; looking back at Jim*)

I was wrong when I told you that staying alive is as good as it gets.

JIM
(*smiles*)

That's what I was thinking.

SELENA

. . . Was it?

JIM

Uh-huh. You stole my thought.

Selena leans over and gives Jim a light kiss on the cheek.

SELENA
(*smiling back at Jim*)

Sorry.

JIM
(*slightly surprised, but pleased*)

Ah, keep it.

EXT. PICNIC SPOT. SUNSET.

Frank switches off the radio. He looks over at Hannah, who is dozing peacefully, then over to Jim and Selena.

> FRANK
> (*calling*)
> It's getting late. We should stay here the night.

Jim raises a hand in reply.

EXT. CAB/PICNIC SPOT. NIGHT.

The cab sits, parked up at the picnic spot. Jim, Selena, Frank and Hannah lie beside it, wrapped in their jackets, using their small backpacks as pillows.

The moon is bright, and only Selena is asleep . . .

> HANNAH
> Can't sleep.

> JIM
> Nor can I. It doesn't feel safe, outdoors like this.

> FRANK
> I think we're safe enough.

A couple of moments pass.

> HANNAH
> . . . Selena didn't seem to have any trouble.

> JIM
> I know. I noticed that too. (*Reaching over and shaking Selena's shoulder.*) Selena . . . Selena!

> SELENA
> (*extremely drowsy*)
> What . . . what is it . . .

> JIM
> How did you manage to get to sleep?

Selena gives a dozy grumble, then sits up, reaches into her backpack, and pulls out several bottles of pills. She hands one of them to Jim.

FRANK

Bloody hell. You must have needed a hell of a prescription for that lot.

SELENA
(*drowsy*)

I didn't need a prescription. I'm a qualified chemist.

She drops back down and goes straight back to sleep.

JIM
(*inspecting the bottle*)

Valium. Great. Not only will it get us to sleep, but if we get attacked during the night, we won't even care. (*Pops the lid.*) Two each?

FRANK

Not for me, thanks.

JIM
(*indicating Hannah*)

What about . . .?

HANNAH

Can I, Dad?

FRANK
(*doubtful*)

I don't know, honey.

HANNAH

Da-ad, plee-ease. I can't sle-eep.

FRANK

All right, all right. Give her half of one.

Fade to:

JIM'S VALIUM DREAM.

Jim is riding his bike through the city. It's London back to normal, pre-infection. Busy streets, traffic, pedestrians, car horns, radios playing.

Jim rides fast, his courier bag over his shoulder, weaving between cars, shooting a red light, turning a corner into . . .

Gower Street. Suddenly, a car pulls out into Jim's path. The car brakes hard, and Jim brakes hard, skidding . . .

. . . and the two miss each other by a whisker.

The Driver flashes into road rage.

> DRIVER

You stupid cunt!

> JIM

Fuck you!

The Driver flips Jim the finger, and accelerates away.

Jim remains stopped by the pavement, one foot down for balance, breathing hard. Pedestrians pass. Groups of people, everyday people, walking by.

Jim watches them, noticing their faces. Some talk to each other, or into mobile phones. Some smile, or walk lost in thought.

After a few moments, Jim sets off again, seemingly distracted, still watching pedestrians' faces . . . then two of the faces seem to catch his attention. A man and a woman, middle-aged, chatting.

His parents.

Jim's head turns as he passes them, confusion on his face, his bike drifting into another lane . . .

. . . into the path of a second car. The car that hit him.

Cut to:

EXT. CAB/PICNIC SPOT. NIGHT.

> FRANK
> (*quietly*)

Hey.

Frank's hand is on Jim's shoulder. Jim stirs, half-wakes.

JIM
(confused, semi-conscious)

What . . .

Frank is sitting beside him — and we see for the first time that Frank is awake, keeping guard over them while they sleep.

FRANK

Shh. You're having a bad dream, that's all.

Jim's face relaxes a little.

JIM
(mumbled, half-asleep already)

Okay, Dad.

Frank raises his eyebrows, then smiles.

EXT. CAB/PICNIC SPOT. EARLY MORNING.

Jim is sitting up. The others are all awake. Frank bouncing the repaired flat tyre to check it, Hannah slipping on a fresh sweatshirt from her backpack, Selena leaning against the cab, chewing on a chocolate bar.

JIM

Here you go, Frank. This is how you catch dew. I'm covered in the fucking stuff.

FRANK
(packing the spare away)

Okay. Let's get rolling. (*He checks his watch.*) If we make good time, we'll be there before midday.

EXT. MOTORWAY. DAY.

The cab is driving, towards us, then slows to a halt.

INT. CAB. DAY.

Everyone is looking at something ahead of them. They seem awestruck.

JIM

Bloody hell . . .

FRANK

It must be Manchester.

JIM

But, the whole of Manchester. The whole city . . .

SELENA

No fire crews to put it out.

We see what they are looking at . . .

EXT. CAB. DAY.

On the horizon ahead, there is the glow of a truly massive fire. The smoke spreads into the sky like the plume from a vast, spreading volcano crater. The city burning.

INT. CAB. DAY.

The cab drives towards the surreal sight. As they drive, pale flakes begin to fall, drifting past the windows.

JIM

It can't be . . .

HANNAH

Is it snow?

FRANK
(*hitting the windscreen wipers*)

It's ash.

EXT. CAB. DAY. ASH FALL.

The cab drives through the ash fall. Through the soft blizzard, they pass a sign for: MANCHESTER − 14 MILES (*in the opposite lane*). *The city is behind them.*

EXT. MOTORWAY. DAY. ASH FALL.

The cab drives down a motorway. The ash is still falling, and they start to pass bodies by the roadside.

INT. CAB. DAY. ASH FALL.

Inside the cab there is a sense of real anticipation. Everyone is sat up, scanning the road ahead.

Then they come over the brow of a hill, and the ash-fall clears like mist parting, to reveal . . .

> FRANK
> Okay, everyone. I think this is it.

EXT. MOTORWAY. DAY.

Fifty metres down, the road is blockaded. It is obviously a military construction – hurriedly put together, but expertly built.

Behind rolls of razor wire are fifteen foot sheets of corrugated iron, held upright by scaffold pipes. In the middle of the blockade there is a gap wide enough to get a vehicle through, but concrete blocks force a chicane.

On either side of the road there are sandbag nests. On the corrugated iron, white painted words read: 42ND BLOCKADE. *But despite the impressive construction, there is no sign of movement or life.*

INT. CAB. DAY.

> JIM
> Try the horn.

> SELENA
> Don't. We might attract the wrong kind of attention.

EXT. 42ND BLOCKADE. DAY.

The cab rolls slowly towards the blockade – past many more bodies, Infected, rotting.

It reaches the chicane, and eases around the concrete blocks. Then it passes through the gap in the corrugated barrier. On the other side of the blockade, canvas tents have been erected on the grass verge, and two transporter trucks are parked. A few packing crates and tarpaulins are also scattered around. But still no signs of life. The blockade appears to have been abandoned.

Frank slows to a halt, but keeps the engine running.

INT. CAB. DAY.

FRANK

What do you think?

JIM

It looks deserted.

SELENA

Or overrun.

Frank flicks the radio on – there is only static. He switches it off again.

FRANK

Let's check it out.

EXT. 42ND BLOCKADE. DAY.

Everyone exits the cab, holding their various weapons. Jim has his baseball bat, Selena has her machete, and Frank has his lead pipe . . .

Cautiously, they begin to explore. They first head over to the grass verge and the tents. In front of one of them, Hannah picks up a Bergen backpack. She upends it, and a few clothes fall out.

Frank moves past her, and carefully pulls back the tent flaps – machete at the ready. Inside, there is a small table, and maps and papers are strewn across the floor. And a radio.

HANNAH

I don't understand. Did they leave?

Jim pushes open the flaps of another tent with his baseball bat.

JIM

They didn't all leave.

Inside, several body bags lie, buzzing with flies.

Selena stands several feet away, by one of the packing cases. She pulls out a tangle of camouflage webbing, then lets it drop back inside.

SELENA

I don't like this. I think we should go.

FRANK
(*suddenly snapping*)
No! (*He composes himself.*) The vehicles. We should check the vehicles first. There has to be something . . .

EXT. VEHICLES. DAY.

Frank jumps down from the back of one of the trucks. Like the others, like everything else, it is empty.

FRANK
Nothing. Nothing here. I can't believe it.

SELENA

Frank.

FRANK

'We should go.'

SELENA

Yes.

FRANK
(*exploding*)

Go fucking where? What the fuck are we supposed to do?
How is this going to fucking end? *It's never going to –*

Frank cuts himself off. Then, turning from the others, he walks away.

EXT. BLOCKADE. DAY.

*Frank walks underneath the archway of one of the blockade
structures, and sits down. Needing to be alone.*

*His head sinks, staring at the ground beneath his legs. A couple of
moments later he looks up – and sees that sat opposite him, on the
other side of the archway, almost mirroring his posture and position,
is a dead Infected.*

The corpse of the Infected sits gazing back at Frank with sightless eyes.

A moment between the two of them. A blank-faced exchange.

Frank looks left and sees the corpse of another Infected, a few feet beyond the blockade. And another, beyond it. And another, a few more feet to the right.

Then Frank looks upwards. Above him, on the walkway of the blockade, another corpse lies. And this corpse is swarmed with crows, picking at it.

Frank gets up.

> FRANK
> (*under his breath*)
> Get out of it. (*then suddenly shouting*) GET OUT OF IT!

The crows ignore him.

He bends, picks up a rock and throws it, but it misses, sailing past them.

In a rage again, Frank goes under the blockade and starts to kick it. The scaffold clangs, vibrates, and – startled – the crows lift off from the mutilated corpse and fly . . .

. . . dislodging, or disrupting, a single droplet of blood from the corpse, that rolls off the neck, and begins to fall downwards.

Down . . . to where Frank gazes upwards.

The droplet splashes, pinpoint perfect, on Frank's eye.

Frank frowns, his hand immediately going to his face. The fingers come away, with the tiny smear of red.

> HANNAH
> Dad . . . are you okay?

Frank turns. Hannah is there, with Jim. Selena stands a little way further back.

> FRANK
> I . . . I'm fine, honey. I'm sorry. I just lost my temper. I . . .

He breaks off.

HANNAH

. . . What?

Frank frowns. A hand goes to his temple.

FRANK

Hannah . . .

Abruptly, the colour is draining from his face.

FRANK
(*continuing, to Hannah*)

Get away from me.

HANNAH

. . . Dad?

FRANK

Get away from me! (*to Jim*) Get her away from me!

HANNAH
(*moving to Frank*)

Why? What's . . .

Frank lashes out and shoves Hannah away, knocking her back to the ground.

FRANK

GET AWAY FROM ME!

A trickle of blood runs out of Frank's nose. Then he doubles up, clutching the side of his head. He screams with pain.

SELENA

Jim . . . (*breaking into a run*) Jim, he's infected!

HANNAH

No! No!

Hannah lunges towards her dad, but is caught by Selena.

SELENA
(*holding Hannah back*)

Jim!

But Jim is frozen, holding his baseball bat.

Frank screams again. Then drops to his knees.

Hannah struggles with Selena, trying to get to Frank.

> HANNAH
>
> Dad!

> SELENA
>
> Jim!

Jim is still frozen, baseball bat half-raised.

> KILL HIM!

And Frank looks up, his face contorted. The infection has taken hold.

And at that moment there is a rifle report, a rush of air, and a rapid thump of impact.

Frank falls forwards to the tarmac.

A moment of silence.

> HANNAH
>
> . . . Dad?

Selena lets Hannah go.

Suddenly, the gunfire comes again. Three shots in quick succession – into Frank's motionless body.

In a daze, Hannah starts towards her dead father.

> CLIFTON
>
> STAY AWAY FROM HIM!

They all turn to see three British soldiers standing by a jeep. One of the soldiers (Farrell) advances, with his gun still raised, while the others (Mitchell and Clifton) hold back, giving cover.

> FARRELL
>
> Get away from the man! NOW!

Jim steps towards Hannah and grabs her, pulling her away from Frank's body. She doesn't struggle. She is in a state of absolute shock.

> SELENA
> (*quietly*)

Jesus.

EXT. ROAD. DAY.

*A jeep drives down a small road – away from the blockade. Jim,
Selena and Hannah sit in the back. Behind is the cab, driven by the
Sergeant. A little way ahead of them, the walled grounds of a huge
country mansion appear.*

EXT. FRONT DRIVEWAY. DAY.

*From a cast-iron-gated entrance, a gravel driveway leads up to the
impressive country mansion, surrounded by a high perimeter wall. The
grounds show acres of lawn and flower beds. These have obviously had
many years of very careful cultivation and attention, but now are just
starting to look unkempt and overgrown.*

*The jeep pulls up by the front steps. Waiting there is another soldier,
a major. Like the other soldiers, he is unshaven, but has the authority
of command about him, even in the relaxed way that he stands.*

*As Jim, Selena and Hannah dismount from the jeep, he appraises
them. Then speaks.*

> HENRY

I'm Major Henry West. Welcome. We've got beds with clean
sheets and a boiler that produces hot water. So you can all
have a shower. You look like you need one.

Jim, Selena, and tear-streaked Hannah gaze back at Henry blankly.

INT. SHOWER. DAY.

*Jim has a shower, sees the cab driving round in circles outside the
shower window, then . . .*

INT. MANSION. DAY.

Jim walks down a sweeping staircase to the front hall. Scattered around are various bits of military gear. A pair of muddy boots, a jacket, assorted kit, webbing, etc.

EXT. VERANDA. DAY.

Henry is sat, looking out over the back lawn.

Pulling back, we see Jim is with him.

> HENRY
>
> You heard our broadcast.

> JIM
>
> Yes.

> HENRY
>
> We must be a disappointment. You were hoping for a full brigade. An army base, with helicopters and field hospitals.

> JIM
>
> We were hoping for . . .

> HENRY
>
> The answer to infection. Well, as I said, it's here. Though it may not be quite what you imagined.

> JIM
>
> I didn't know what to imagine, so . . . We just feel lucky to have found you.

> HENRY
>
> You were lucky. The fire drove hundreds of infected out of Manchester. The surrounding area is teeming with them.

Henry glances back at Jim.

> But there's no need for you to worry. We're well protected here.

EXT. GARDEN. DAY.

Henry shows Jim around the grounds.

> HENRY
>
> Three-sixty visibility. Flat terrain all round the house . . .
> Floodlights, which we've rigged up to a generator. Don't
> like to waste the fuel, but when we want to, we can turn
> night into day.

Moving on . . .

> High perimeter wall, which helps, and we've been lacing
> the grounds with trip wires and land mines.

*Henry indicates where Farrell, Smith and Davis can be seen, running
a trip wire.*

> You wouldn't want to go mowing the lawn, but if they get
> in, we hear them.

INT. MANSION — LOWER LEVELS. DAY.

Henry leads Jim into the basement level of the mansion.

> HENRY
>
> Secondary to protection, our real job is to rebuild. Start
> again. Down here is the wood-fired boiler that provides us
> with hot water. Our first step to civilization.

Then to a kitchen . . .

> And here, the kitchen.

INT: MANSION — KITCHEN. DAY.

*Several of the soldiers are unpacking the food bags from the cab. One
of the soldiers, Jones, is wearing an apron.*

> HENRY
>
> What are you cooking, Jones?

> JONES
>
> It's a surprise, sir!

EXT. MAILER'S PIT. DAY.

Henry leads Jim into a small courtyard, hanging with bloodstained laundry.

HENRY

And finally . . .

The laundry starts to billow – and with it we hear the sound of rushing movement. As a darkly stained sheet is ripped aside, an Infected is revealed only a few feet away.

Jim jumps back, but Henry stays put – as the Infected is suddenly jerked backwards by a chain around its neck.

. . . meet Mailer.

Mailer is uniformed. A soldier. Apart from the chain around his neck, he is gagged with a filthy and blood-blackened rag tied tight into his mouth.

HENRY

Mailer, Jim. Jim, Mailer. Got infected three days ago. Mitchell managed to knock him out cold. Got a chain around his neck.

JIM

You're keeping him alive?

HENRY

The idea was to learn something about infection. Have him teach me.

JIM

And has he?

HENRY

In a way. (*Kneels.*) He's teaching me he'll never bake bread. Plant crops, raise livestock. He's telling me he's futureless. And eventually he'll tell me how long the infected take to starve to death.

A moment.

Dinner's at seven. Don't forget to tell the girls.

Henry exits, leaving Jim with Mailer.

Mailer lunges at Jim – a moment between them.

Then Jim exits.

INT. GIRLS' BEDROOM. DAY.

Carefully, Jim opens the door to the girls' bedroom. Inside is Hannah, lying on the bed, face covered, on her side. Selena lies behind her, her arm lying protectively over Hannah's body.

Selena looks around, sees Jim, and puts a finger to her lips.

INT. JIM'S BEDROOM. NIGHT.

Jim and Selena enter, and close the door.

>   JIM
> . . . So how is she?

>   SELENA
> She's lost her dad. That's how she is. (*A moment.*) It's all
> fucked, Jim.

Suddenly Selena looks as if she's on the verge of tears.

>   JIM
> Hey, don't . . . do that. Look, Hannah . . . Hannah's what
> Frank said she was. Tough. Strong. And just like me, just
> like you, she will cope . . .

>   SELENA
> Shut up, Jim. Just shut up. I don't want her to fucking *cope*.
> I want her to be *okay*. And when Hannah had her dad,
> it was all okay. Remember? And when it was okay for them,
> it was okay for us. And now it's *all fucked*.

Then Selena's tears are flowing.

Jim seems to want to reply, but doesn't have the words.

Instead, he lifts Selena's face and kisses her on the lips . . .

. . . a moment.

Then Selena pushes him away.

Selena leaves the room.

INT. MANSION — DINING ROOM. NIGHT.

A surreal scene.

Dinner, with full silver service, candles, wine and crystal glasses, napkins, and everyone rather formally sat while Jones lays food on the table, wearing an apron over his uniform.

Made all the more surreal by Jim and Selena's grubby clothes, and Hannah's dazed, tear-streaked face.

> HENRY
>
> So, what have we here? Tinned ham, tinned peas, and omelette. You've prepared a feast, Jones.

> JONES
>
> Honour of our guests, sir.

> HENRY
>
> Absolutely. I was going to suggest a toast, but this omelette will do just as well. (*Cuts off a chunk of omelette and raises it.*) To new friends.

Henry pops the omelette in his mouth, then promptly spits it out.

> Jones, did you notice while cooking that these eggs are off?

> JONES
>
> I thought the salt might cover the taste, sir.

> HENRY
> (*pushing his plate away*)
>
> Get rid of it.

Henry turns to Hannah as Jones sheepishly exits, carrying the omelette.

> I don't suppose you can cook, can you? I can't tell you how badly we need someone who shows a little flair in the kitchen.

Hannah ignores/is unaware of Henry's attempt to bring her out of her shell.

Meanwhile, the soldiers start helping themselves to the other food on the table.

DAVIS

That's a fucking disappointment. When I saw those eggs, I thought it was Christmas.

BELL

We'll have eggs again. Once everything's back to normal.

The soldiers pause. Exchange glances. Then burst out laughing.

MITCHELL

Listen to him! He's still waiting for Marks and Spencer's to reopen.

More laughter at Bell – interrupted by the sergeant, Farrell, who conspicuously is not joining in.

FARRELL

I think Bell's got a point. If you look at the whole life of the planet, man has only been around for a few blinks of an eye. So if the infection wipes us all out, that is a return to normality.

Farrell turns to Bell.

Is that what you meant, Bell?

BELL

Uh . . . yeah.

HENRY
(*to Jim and Selena*)

Have you met our new-age sergeant? (*to Farrell*) Remind me, Farrell, why exactly did you join the army in the first place?

A moment.

This is what I've seen in the four weeks since infection. People killing people. Which is much what I saw in the four

79

weeks before infection, and the four weeks before that, and before that, as far back as I care to remember . . . People killing people. Which to my mind puts us in a state of normality right now.

Selena turns to Hannah.

> SELENA
> (*quiet*)
>
> You're not eating.

> HANNAH
>
> I don't want to eat.

Henry picks up on their exchange.

> HENRY
>
> You must eat, Hannah.

> HANNAH
>
> I don't want to eat. I want to bury my dad. He's one of the people you're talking about.

A silence over the dinner table.

Broken by the thud of a mine detonation.

Then . . .

> FARRELL
>
> Stand to!

And suddenly all the soldiers are kicking back their chairs, jumping to their feet. Producing SA-80s that they had under the table.

EXT. MANSION. DAY.

Farrell, Jones, Mitchell, Bedford, Smith and Clifton race out of the house, fanning, dropping into position.

> MITCHELL
>
> Go, go, go!

Two more soldiers, Davis and Bell, fire from window positions on the mansion's first floor.

FARRELL

Jones! Cover right!

SMITH

Three o'clock! Three o'clock!

Coming across the grounds are four Infected, sprinting across the lawn towards the house. Immediately, one of them is catapulted into the air by an explosion under its feet – a mine.

The soldiers open fire, Jones closing his eyes as he pulls the trigger.

The three remaining Infected are cut down – one hit in the head by Smith, another folding under a burst from Farrell, the last falling under fire from Mitchell, landing face down on a mine which explodes onto its chest.

Chunks of Infected spin into the air, then patter down like a light rain.

MITCHELL
(*delighted*)

That was mad! Did you see that! That was fucking mad!

FARRELL
(*angry*)

Clear!

JONES

Clear.

MITCHELL
(*still laughing*)

Clear. (*to Jones*) Fuck me, I never saw that before. Keeled over and – bam! Gone, like fucking magic.

SMITH

I drew a lovely bead. One shot. Right between its eyes.

INT. LIVING ROOM. DAY.

Jim stands, looking out of the open French windows at the soldiers.

Selena is standing behind him. She is holding her machete.

The soldiers bounce in. Mitchell and Smith in particular are hyped from their adrenaline rush.

> MITCHELL

It was all hanging in the air, and all these bits coming down, and . . .

Mitchell catches sight of Selena holding her machete.

Hello.

He heads towards her, and takes the machete from her hands.

I'll tell you what: you don't need this penknife any more, sweetie. I'm here to protect you now. (*Winks at the other soldiers.*) But listen, if you want to hold a huge chopper . . .

Bedford bursts out laughing, and Selena grabs her machete back.

Whoa! Feisty!

He gives her a slap on the backside.

> SELENA

Fuck you!

> MITCHELL

You bet. How about right now?

Now doubly hyped, Mitchell reaches forward and pulls up the hem of Selena's T-shirt. She yelps and twists, knocking back his hand.

Yeah! A little rough stuff!

> FARRELL

MITCHELL!

But Farrell clearly has little command over Mitchell, who tries again for Selena's T-shirt, still laughing.

Jim snaps.

> JIM
> (*angrily grabbing Mitchell*)

Cut it out!

And Mitchell turns immediately on Jim, his sexual charge flipping seamlessly back to violence.

MITCHELL
(grabbing Jim, propelling him back across the room, up against a wall)
Easy, tiger. You don't want to go picking a fight with me.

Suddenly Farrell is behind Mitchell. We see a movement (a kidney punch), and Mitchell drops.

MITCHELL
(gasping, on the ground)
Ahh, you cunt. Cunt.

Then – as if through sixth sense, sensing a presence, all turn. Henry is standing in the doorway.

A moment. Then Henry turns to Mitchell – who has picked himself up, and is clutching his side, breathing hard.

HENRY
Corporal, first point of order after an attack.

MITCHELL
Re-secure the perimeter, sir.

HENRY
Then get to it. Jones, Bedford, go with him. *(to Farrell)*
Sergeant.

FARRELL
(tightly)
Sir.

HENRY
Clear the bodies off the lawn. The rest of you go with him.

The soldiers exit, leaving only Jim, Henry and Selena in the room.

Selena is shaken, and won't meet Jim's eyes.

Henry hands Selena her machete back.

My apologies.

Selena takes the machete and exits, but Jim doesn't follow. Obviously there is something he wants to say to Henry.

INT. LIVING ROOM. NIGHT.

Jim and Henry enter the living room.

HENRY

Drink?

Henry walks over to a drinks cabinet, and pours two brandies, waiting for Jim to speak.

JIM

Look. We're grateful. Very grateful for your protection, and just to have found other people. But if we're going to stay here with you, you're going to have stop your men from –

HENRY

Who have you killed?

JIM
(*thrown*)

I haven't killed anyone.

Henry hands Jim his drink.

HENRY

Since it began, who have you killed? You wouldn't be alive now if you hadn't killed somebody.

A moment.

JIM

A boy. I killed a boy.

HENRY

A child?

JIM

Yes.

HENRY

But you had to. Otherwise he'd have killed you. Survival. I understand. (*Beat.*) I promised them women.

JIM

What?

84

HENRY

Eight days ago I found Jones with his gun in his mouth. He said he was going to kill himself because there was no future. What could I say to him? We kill all the infected or wait until they starve to death. And then what? What do nine men do except wait to die themselves? (*Beat.*) I moved us from the blockade, I set the radio broadcasting, and I promised them women. Because women mean children.

Jim turns and runs out of the room.

And children mean a future.

INT. GIRLS' BEDROOM. NIGHT.

Jim bursts into the girls' bedroom. Selena is dressed, sat next to Hannah, who is awake.

JIM

Get up. Get up!

SELENA

Wha . . .

JIM

We've got to get out of here!

SELENA

But we . . .

JIM
(*hauling them up*)
We're leaving. Now! NOW!

INT. MANSION STAIRS. NIGHT.

Jim and the girls run down the stairs . . .

. . . heading for the front door.

But behind it is Mitchell, waiting, holding his SA-80.

Jim is hit full in the face, and blacks out.

As he comes round, he can hear the sound of shouting and screaming.

Farrell is backing away from the other soldiers, who are closing in on him, even though his gun is raised.

FARRELL

You can't do this! You can't do this! Get back! I'll fucking slot you! I'll slot you, I fucking swear it!

But he doesn't follow his threat through. We hear him scream as the soldiers overpower him.

Jim looks up, and sees Henry is kneeling over him.

HENRY

I want to give you a chance. You can be with us, or not.

Jim stares back at him. And Henry gazes at Jim, searching behind Jim's eyes. And understands what he finds.

Okay, Jim. Okay.

Henry gives Jim's cheek a soft pat, then rises.

HENRY
(*continuing, to Mitchell*)

Him too.

Jim's eyes flick to the side, where he sees Selena holding Hannah tightly.

Selena looks down at Jim, terrified.

Black screen.

FARRELL'S VOICE

He's insane.

INT. CELLAR.

Jim, blindfolded, is sat beside a radiator, to which his hands are tied.

He is in a cellar. Farrell is on the other side of the small room, also tied.

Jim, blind, looks around at the sound of Farrell's voice.

FARRELL

You know what they're doing, a few hundred miles from here? Across the channel, across the Atlantic, they're eating dinner. They're wondering what to watch on TV tonight. They're sleeping next to their wives.

Jim's head turns.

FARRELL

But we're here, chained to a fucking radiator because the OC has gone insane. Starting the world again when the rest of the world hasn't even fucking stopped. Think about it! How could infection cross the oceans? How could it cross the mountains and the rivers? They stopped it. And right now TVs are playing and planes are flying in the sky and the world is continuing as fucking normal. Think. Actually think about it. What would you do with a diseased little island?

A moment.

They quarantined us.

A moment.

FARRELL
(*continuing; quiet*)

There is no infection. It's just people killing people. (*Beat.*) He's insane.

JIM

. . . Quarantine?

Then the door to the cellar bursts open, revealing Mitchell and Jones.

EXT. TREE-LINED PATH. DAY.

Mitchell and Jones are leading Jim and Farrell through a small forest at the back of the mansion garden.

Time has passed. It has started raining. Both Jim and Farrell have been badly beaten. Jim's shirt is ripped. Blood runs from his nose, and from a cut on the side of his head. He seems dazed. Numbed. More by the situation than his beating.

87

EXT. EXECUTION GROUND. DAY.

*Jim and Farrell are led into a clearing. Just ahead is a high,
ivy-covered brick wall – the perimeter wall of the mansion. And at the
base of the wall are bodies. Stacked, tangled, swarming with flies.*

Jim turns, and sees Mitchell and Jones standing behind him.

> FARRELL
> Come on then, you fucking pansies. Do me first.

Mitchell grins, and pulls out his bayonet.

> So you're going to stick me, Mitchell? Is that it? (*to Jones*)
> Is that how you're going to let your sergeant go out, Jones?

JONES

No, Mitch. Do it with the gun.

Mitchell ignores Jones, and starts to fix the blade to the end of his gun.

FARRELL

You're going to let him stick me, are you? Like a fucking dog?

JONES

Mitch, come on. Just shoot him.

MITCHELL

Why?

JONES

Because it's quick.

MITCHELL

So?

The bayonet fixes home with a click.

JONES

I'll shoot him, then.

MITCHELL

You fucking won't. (*to Farrell*) Any last words?

Farrell spits in Mitchell's face.

I'm going to enjoy this.

Mitchell pulls back his bayonet, and at that moment, there is an explosion of gunfire. Jones has fired and killed Farrell.

As Farrell drops, the enraged Mitchell turns on Jones.

You stupid cunt! What are you doing?

Mitchell knocks Jones down, putting his gun right in Jones's face.

JONES
(*whirling*)

How did he . . .

They turn. Jim has vanished.

From the side of the clearing, in the trees, there is the sound of sudden movement.

There!

Both men immediately set off, diving back into the foliage . . .

A beat passes. Then, in the pile of bodies, one of them sits up . . .

. . . Jim. We have been looking right at him. But in the tangle of bodies, and the bloodstained clothes, his camouflage was complete.

EXT. TREES. DAY. LIGHT RAIN.

Mitchell and Jones move fast, scanning, pushing through the undergrowth. Mitchell is absolutely furious. And as they run, they startle a couple of birds, which fly up from the ground, making a suspiciously familiar noise . . .

They both have the same realisation at the same moment.

EXT. EXECUTION GROUND. DAY.

Mitchell and Jones burst back into the clearing, and they start firing into the bodies, emptying a full clip into the corpses . . .

. . . Silence.

Then Jones looks up to the ivy-covered wall . . . following the path of the ivy upwards, to the coiled razor wire, where a scrap of torn and bloody clothing hangs.

JONES
Oh no. We're fucked, we're fucked.

MITCHELL
No problem. He's outside. No gun. No vehicle. He's a dead man.

EXT. WOODS. DAY.

Jim runs through the woods, away from the mansion. His hands are still tied.

He is out of breath, frightened, jumping at every sound.

Then he trips, rolls down a short slope, and when he comes to rest, he is looking upwards.

Above him, there is a parting in the clouds, and through the parting is blue sky.

And across the sky, bisecting the blue, is a single vapour trail.

A pin-prick of silver plane. Followed by a sonic boom. As much in Jim's head as anywhere else.

Cut to:

INT. DOOR. DAY.

Close-up of a closed door, with the sounds of a struggle on the other side.

Then, suddenly, Selena's voice: hard, desperate:

> SELENA
> You can't do this to her! She's only fourteen!

INT. DRESSING ROOM. DAY. RAIN.

Note: in the room is a large, freestanding mirror.

Hannah and Selena are cornered by Clifton, Bedford, Bell and Davis. The soldiers are hyped. Bedford pulls clothes out of a wardrobe, yanking out dresses, underwear – throwing them at the girls.

Bell stands by the closed door – frightened, caught like a rabbit in the headlights between the testosterone madness and the horror.

And Clifton is laughing, animal-like, tearing at Selena's clothes, while Hannah is kicking and screaming – held by Davis.

Close-up on Selena: suddenly transfixed by Hannah the young girl's fight, the hopelessness.

Abruptly, Selena turns, grabs Clifton's arm, and to his amazement, yanks him around.

Then she kisses him on the lips. Simply, but unambiguously.

Bell, Davis and Bedford watch in amazement.

Selena breaks off.

The frenzy has been broken by her extraordinary action – and bizarrely, so has the balance of power.

> SELENA
> You need to give me a moment with Hannah. Alone.

Clifton nods – he seems a little dazed.

> CLIFTON
> The OC. He . . . he wants you to . . .

> SELENA
> He wants us to dress up nice.

She picks up two of the dresses Bedford has thrown – the red dresses.

> But if you want us to change, you'll have to get out of the room.

A moment.

> SELENA
> *(continuing, calm, powerful)*
> It's just fucking polite.

Another moment.

Then Clifton nods. Acquiesces.

> CLIFTON
> *(to the others)*
> Okay. Clear out.

They exit.

Selena stands with Hannah, emptying pills from her Valium bottle.

> SELENA
> Eat them.

Hannah hesitates.

SELENA
(*continuing, hard*)
Eat them, Hannah!

Hannah takes the handful of pills and holds them in her open palm.

Then she looks to Selena.

HANNAH
Are you killing me?

A moment – maybe a single moment of tenderness, a strand of hair brushed from Hannah's face.

SELENA
No. I'm making you not care.

Locked eyes with Selena, Hannah raises the first pill to her mouth. Then the next.

The door behind opens – revealing the soldiers.

Clifton sees what is happening.

CLIFTON
Hey! What the fuck are you doing?

Selena crams the pills into Hannah's mouth.

The soldiers lunge for the girls, as Hannah tries to swallow the pills, and Selena whirls to fight them off . . .

. . . and at that moment, the sound of a distant siren begin to rise.

Everyone freezes.

Then . . .

SELENA
Jim.

BEDFORD
He's at the blockade!

INT: MANSION — STAIRS. DAY. RAIN.

The soldiers run down the stairs.

> JONES
> He went over the wall! We thought he'd be dead sir!

> HENRY
> Shut up! Davis – you're coming with me!

EXT: BLOCKADE. DAY. RAIN.

Jim stands in the blockade, turning the handle of a siren. Rain is pouring down, mingling with the blood on his face.

Jim stops, and the sound of the siren starts to fade away.

From the motorway ahead, through the rain, a jeep is approaching.

EXT. MOTORWAY. LATE AFTERNOON. RAIN.

The jeep drives fast down the motorway, and pulls up. Davis is driving and Henry stands on the back, manning the jeep's mounted machine gun.

The jeep pulls up, one hundred metres from the blockade, and Henry brings the mounted machine gun to bear on the blockade.

> HENRY
> Okay. Let's see if we can sidestep the cat-and-mouse bullshit.

Henry opens fire.

EXT. BLOCKADE. LATE AFTERNOON. RAIN.

Bullets rip through the blockade, punching holes through the vehicles, smashing through the packing crates . . .

EXT. MOTORWAY. LATE AFTERNOON. RAIN.

Henry stops shooting. With a peal of thunder, the rain suddenly begins to flood down.

The barrel of the machine gun spits and steams as the raindrops hit the hot metal.

EXT. BLOCKADE. LATE AFTERNOON. HEAVY RAIN.

Davis pulls up at the outskirts of the blockade, and they get out of the truck.

Henry and Davis make their way into the blockade. With a signal from Henry, the two split up.

EXT. BLOCKADE — WITH HENRY. LATE AFTERNOON. HEAVY RAIN.

Henry moves through the blockade.

He lets off a controlled burst of shots into the tents.

EXT. BLOCKADE — WITH DAVIS. LATE AFTERNOON. HEAVY RAIN.

Stealthily, Davis searches around the trucks and tents . . .

A flash of movement – fast, like an Infected, ducking behind one of the trucks: Jim.

Davis wipes the rain from his eyes, and presses forwards.

Jim is nowhere to be seen.

Another flash of movement, around the back of the next truck.

Davis moves around the truck . . . but Jim is not there.

DAVIS

Fuck.

Davis turns, and sees . . .

. . . Jim, flying towards him, holding Frank's lead pipe, lips drawn back over his teeth in a rictus smile, murderous.

He is the vision of the Infected, in his expression, his movements, the blood, everything.

EXT. BLOCKADE — WITH HENRY. LATE AFTERNOON. HEAVY RAIN.

Henry turns, as if having just heard something. Perhaps a scream.

> HENRY
> (*calling*)
> Jim?

Another noise. This time it is unambiguously an Infected howl. Henry turns again. From down the motorway, and from the fields, he can now see the Infected. A large number, attracted by the noise of the heavy machine gun, are approaching.

He looses off a couple of shots at the Infected, then starts to back away to the jeep.

EXT. JEEP. LATE AFTERNOON. HEAVY RAIN.

Henry runs up to the jeep. Through the rain, and the water running down the windscreen, Henry can see a figure sat at the driver's seat.

> HENRY
> Davis?

The figure doesn't move.

Henry approaches cautiously, gun raised, and finds . . .

. . . Davis sat on the front seat, dead, his skull smashed open.

Henry whirls, expecting to find Jim behind him.

But there is no one there.

Henry shoots again, blindly, emptying his clip at anything and everything around him.

He reloads – hurriedly, hands slipping on the wet clip, betraying nervousness . . .

. . . and fires at a rain shadow that sweeps between two of the tents. Then his nerve is gone.

> HENRY
> (*continuing*)
> Fine! Fine, you little bastard! Fucking die out here!

Henry hauls out Davis's body, gets into the driver's seat, turning the ignition . . .

. . . but nothing is happening.

Henry turns the key again, desperately. The motor doesn't even turn over.

Reaching under the dashboard, he pulls out a handful of wires.

HENRY
(*continuing*)

Jim.

And at that moment, an Infected slams onto the windscreen, face against the glass.

Henry shouts out of surprise and anger, lifting his gun, and fires at point-blank range, through the glass, into the Infected's face.

The windscreen shatters, blown outwards.

And now, where our view was obscured by rain-washed glass, we can see clearly . . .

. . . Infected, in the blockade, coming through the downpour, running towards the jeep.

Henry opens fire and cuts them down.

EXT. MAILER'S PIT — NIGHT. RAIN.

Jim appears above Mailer in his pit, and shoots off Mailer's chain.

INT. LIVING ROOM. NIGHT. HEAVY RAIN.

Jones stands holding his gun at Selena and Hannah, who sit on the sofas, opposite each other. Also in the room are Clifton, standing by the French windows, and Mitchell.

Jones seems jumpy, a sheen of sweat on his forehead, as if sensing that things have gone seriously wrong.

A flicker of lightning lights up outside.

JONES

What was that? Was that a claymore?

MITCHELL

It was lightning.

JONES

But I heard something.

A moment. Rain and wind lash the windows.

MITCHELL

I'll go and hit the floods. Take a butcher's. Girls, keep an eye on him, would you?

Mitchell exits.

Jones wipes at the beads of sweat on his upper lip. And in noticeable contrast, Hannah is completely calm . . .

HANNAH

Those pills. I think they're having an effect. I can feel them, and . . . I don't feel sleepy, but . . .

Her sentence trails off. Then she turns to Jones.

HANNAH
(*continuing, to Jones*)

They've been a long time.

Jones says nothing.

What are you going to do if they don't come back?

Jones still says nothing, but the question is clearly hitting a nerve.

Will you be the boss if Henry is dead? Is that the way it works?

Selena looks at Hannah quickly.

JONES

Shut up.

HANNAH

I don't think they are coming back. I think they've been killed.

99

JONES

I told you to shut up!

SELENA
(nervous)

Hannah . . .

HANNAH
(flat)

They're dead.

Hannah's eyes flick over Jones's shoulder, and something fleeting passes over her face.

You're going to be next.

At that moment, a mine detonates in the mansion grounds.

JONES

Shit!

At that moment, the floodlights power up . . .

. . . illuminating Mailer, just on the other side of the French windows, just behind Clifton, a split second before he smashes through.

Then he does smash through.

Clifton is thrown to the ground, with Mailer on top of him.

CLIFTON

Help! Shoot him! Shoot him!

Jones is hopeless, panicking – fires, and misses.

Hannah watches, spaced out. Selena shakes Hannah by the shoulders, pulling Hannah upwards.

SELENA

Hannah! *Hannah!* We have to get out of here!

Mailer vomits blood into Clifton's face.

INT. HALLWAY. NIGHT. RAIN.

Selena and Hannah back out of the living room, through the house. Hannah is very doped up.

SELENA
Oh Jesus, Jesus, Hannah, stay with it, stay with it.

HANNAH
(*relaxed, as she's yanked along*)
Don't worry. I feel fine. Really.

They reach the front hallway, and the front door bursts open . . .

Mitchell, with Bedford.

MITCHELL
What the fuck's going on? What's all the shouti . . .

Mitchell is cut off by a high scream, from down the hall, in the direction of the living room.

All turn, and see . . .

. . . Jones, running, screaming, out of one doorway, across the hallway. He has lost his weapon – and is chased by Mailer, but not Clifton. Like a train passing, in half a second they are out of sight.

A moment. Then Mitchell explodes.

MITCHELL
(*continuing, to Bedford*)
Don't just fucking stand there! *Get after them!*

INT. KITCHEN. NIGHT. HEAVY RAIN.

Mailer chases Jones into the kitchen, but when he enters, Jones is nowhere to be seen.

Mailer turns, and sees Bedford in the kitchen doorway, holding his gun.

BEDFORD
What the fuck are you going to do now, eh?

But just as Bedford lifts his gun to shoot Mailer . . .

Clifton runs at him, full speed from down the corridor . . .

. . . and Bedford is knocked sideways by the infected Clifton.

EXT. MANSION. NIGHT. HEAVY RAIN.

Jim is at the kitchen window, looking in as Bedford is killed by Mailer and Clifton.

INT. CUPBOARD. NIGHT. HEAVY RAIN.

Jones cowers inside a cupboard, hearing Bedford's screams.

INT. MANSION – STAIRS. NIGHT. HEAVY RAIN.

MITCHELL
(grabbing Selena)

Up! Up!

Mitchell pushes the girls up the stairs. At the top of the staircase, wide-eyed with fear, is Bell.

BELL

Mitchell? What's going on?

MITCHELL

Stay here and defend these stairs with your fucking life!

He turns back to the girls, still holding Selena's arm, and Hannah is gone.

Selena sees her, heading away down towards the corridor.

SELENA

Hannah!

Mitchell starts pulling Selena in the opposite direction from Hannah.

INT. DRESSING ROOM. NIGHT. HEAVY RAIN.

Hannah runs into the dressing room.

The freestanding mirror sits in the middle of the floor.

Also on the floor are her clothes, and she starts to look through them, looking for her jeans . . .

. . . which she lifts up, then digs in the pocket, and pulls out . . . a photo of her with Frank and her mother.

She gazes at the photo.

At that moment, there is a noise from behind her.

She looks up, and sees, in the reflection of the mirror, Clifton, running down the corridor towards her.

With Clifton: we burst into the dressing room, which is now empty.

Clifton freezes, then looks around.

And the camera pulls back, to reveal Hannah, clinging on to the back of the large mirror, trembling.

A moment – then Clifton moves on.

INT. KITCHEN. NIGHT. HEAVY RAIN.

Silence in the kitchen. Bedford lies dead, torn to pieces.

A cupboard creaks slowly open, and Jones peers out. He has been hiding.

Trembling with fear, he crawls out . . . moves into the kitchen . . . peers out into the hall.

It is empty.

Jones starts running. Down the corridor outside the kitchen.

INT. FRONT HALL. NIGHT. HEAVY RAIN.

Jones runs into the front hall . . .

And suddenly stops. Dead in his tracks.

Jim is standing right in front of him.

Jones looks surprised, wide eyed. His mouth opens, but no sound comes out.

Pull back, to see: Jones has run straight into Jim's bayonet.

Jones falls, taking the gun and bayonet with him.

Jim steps over his body, and into the house . . .

INT. RADIO ROOM. NIGHT. HEAVY RAIN.

Jim runs through the radio room.

In the break between two blasts of lightning, the room goes dark.

When it is re-illuminated, Jim has gone, and Mailer and Clifton have entered.

INT. MANSION — STAIRS. NIGHT. HEAVY RAIN.

Jim runs up the stairs.

EXT. MANSION. NIGHT. HEAVY RAIN.

Henry walks into the front hall, where he finds Jones.

Jones is lying flat on his back, mortally wounded, gazing up. Still alive – but only just. Taking his very last breaths.

Henry kneels beside him, and Jones's eyes turn to his officer. He blinks, tries to speak, but is too weak and close to death to form the words.

Henry's hand closes around Jones.

Jones blinks once more. And dies.

INT. MANSION — CORRIDOR. NIGHT. HEAVY RAIN.

Jim runs down a corridor.

He tries a door. Locked.

> JIM
> Hannah! Selena!

He tries another door. Open.

He runs through . . .

INT. CHILD'S BEDROOM. NIGHT. HEAVY RAIN

. . . into a kid's bedroom.

Jim moves a sofa to block the doorway – which, as it is moved, reveals . . .

. . . Bell, hiding, cowering, terrified. Foetal.

BELL
(*whimpering*)

I don't have any bullets! I don't have any fucking bullets!

Mailer and Clifton outside try to force their way through, and the sofa jumps forwards an inch.

An Infected arm flails through the half-open door.

Jim leaves Bell, and climbs out the window.

As Jim exits, the door to the room bursts open.

BELL
(*screaming*)

Don't leave me!

EXT. LEDGE. NIGHT. HEAVY RAIN.

Jim climbs along the outside ledge, around the corner of the building.

Behind him, we can hear Bell screaming as he is killed.

Jim keeps going until he reaches the slope of the mansion's pitched roof.

There, he finds a skylight window.

INT. MANSION – BASEMENT CORRIDOR. NIGHT. HEAVY RAIN.

Henry moves into a basement corridor.

Then pauses.

There is the sound of movement.

An Infected howl.

Then suddenly, pouring out from every door and shadow ahead, come a rush of Infected.

Henry opens fire, a volley into them as he backs away fast . . .

. . . to a door, which he slams and bolts behind him.

INT. CORRIDOR. NIGHT. HEAVY RAIN.

Mitchell is holding Selena in one hand, and his gun in the other, dragging her down a corridor.

The howls of the Infected fill the house.

> SELENA

Hannah!

> MITCHELL

Shut your fucking mouth! You want to get us killed?

Mitchell opens a door . . .

. . . which leads nowhere. The floor of the room through the open door is missing.

And below, in the basement-level corridor, the space is full of the Infected.

They look up at Mitchell, and Mitchell looks down at them.

A vision of writhing Hell. They are a mass of faces and bodies. Some are appallingly wounded. Some are half-dressed in ragged clothes. Some are naked.

> MITCHELL
> (*continuing*)

. . . Shit.

He pulls Selena away, towards another door.

In here! IN HERE!

INT. MANSION – BASEMENT CORRIDOR. NIGHT. HEAVY RAIN.

Henry is in the basement corridor, on the other side of the door he has bolted.

Ahead, there is movement – rapid.

Henry looks to the source, and sees: Clifton, running from the front hall towards him, clearly infected.

No alarm registers on Henry's face.

As Clifton sprints towards him, Henry remains still. Then, at the last moment he closes his eyes . . .

. . . and fires.

Clifton is hit, falls.

Henry opens his eyes.

INT. ATTIC. NIGHT. HEAVY RAIN.

Jim enters the skylight window, into an attic, positioned above the girls' bedroom.

In the floor is a hole, and through it he can see Mitchell and Selena.

INT. GIRLS' BEDROOM. NIGHT. HEAVY RAIN.

Selena and Mitchell stand in the middle of the room.

In the room are Selena and Hannah's bags, and Selena's machete, lying by the side of the bed. She can see it, but . . .

. . . Mitchell is holding her tight. He has his gun trained on the door, facing away from the window.

> MITCHELL
> It's me and you, now. And I'm going to get you out of here, and then we're going to find some nice little fucking place, with a pretty little fucking garden, and . . .

Jim drops down from the attic.

Mitchell turns, but is knocked off balance by Selena squirming out of his grip . . . then Jim is on him.

With incredible viciousness, the power and savagery of the infected, Jim beats Mitchell to death. He smashes his head against the wall. Then he throws Mitchell to the ground, and jams his thumbs in Mitchell's eyes.

When it is over, Jim looks up.

Selena stands, holding her machete. She is frozen by the sight of him. The blood on his face. The matted hair. He is the image of an infected.

Jim stands and takes a step towards her. Selena remains, motionless, watching him approach.

Then, just as he is about to reach her, her arm flashes upwards, holding the machete, to cut Jim down . . .

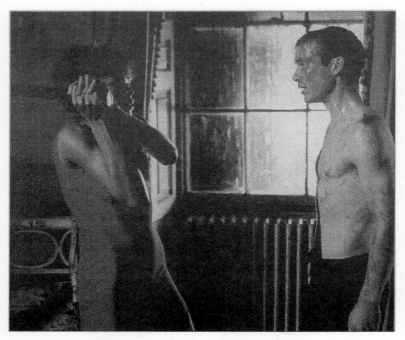

. . . but she hesitates. She can't do it.

A moment. Then . . .

JIM
That was longer than a heartbeat.

SELENA

. . . Jim?

*Jim moves forwards, and kisses her. Simply. Hard. Then pulls back,
leaving a trace of blood on her lips.*

*Behind Jim's back, the door opposite, in the corridor, silently swings
open.*

I thought . . . I thought you were . . .

Jim moves forwards, and they kiss. Passionately.

Then Jim breaks off.

JIM

Listen to me. I've got to tell you – I've got to tell you. The
world isn't fucked. It's going to be okay. We've got a chance,
if we can get to . . .

Selena interrupts him, by continuing the kiss.

And Jim responds.

As, behind him, a small figure in a red dress slips into the room.

Then a vase smashes over the back of Jim's head.

JIM

Ow!

*He reels back, and Hannah is on him, jumping on his back, hitting
him with her fists.*

SELENA

Hannah! Stop! It's okay!

Hannah breaks off.

He's not infected!

HANNAH

I thought he was biting you.

JIM
(*holding the back of his head*)
I was kissing her! (*Breaks off.*) Are you stoned?

SELENA

It's a long story.

They are interrupted by the sounds of Infected howling.

We have to get out of here.

INT. MANSION. NIGHT. HEAVY RAIN.

Jim, Selena and Hannah run out the house, through the front hall, to the cab.

Hannah gets in the driver's seat . . .

. . . and Jim yanks open the back door, ready to pile into the back – only to find . . .

. . . Henry. Sat on the fold-down back seat. Holding his gun.

HENRY

You killed all my boys.

Henry pulls the trigger – a single shot. Jim is hit in the stomach and falls backwards into Selena's arms.

SELENA

Jim!

INT. CAB. NIGHT. HEAVY RAIN.

Hannah floors the accelerator.

But instead of going forward, the cab reverses.

EXT. MANSION. NIGHT. HEAVY RAIN.

HENRY

What . . . Hannah! Hannah?

The cab reverses fast, then Hannah slams the brakes. The cab slides to a halt.

An Infected slams against Henry's window.

At that moment, the back windscreen smashes.

The hands of the Infected grab hold of Henry's head.

Hannah watches, turned around in the seat.

Henry screams – and we see it's Mailer's face behind him.

Hannah floors the accelerator again, but this time in forward gear. Henry is sucked out of the back window.

EXT. CAB. NIGHT. HEAVY RAIN.

The cab screeches up to Jim and Selena.

Selena bundles Jim in, and the cab is off in a spray of gravel . . .

INT. FRONT HALLWAY. NIGHT. HEAVY RAIN.

As Henry is killed by Mailer, the silhouettes of the Infected appear in the shadows.

INT. CAB. NIGHT.

The cab races towards the cast-iron front gates of the mansion – and we see they are locked with a chain and padlock.

> SELENA
> We're going to crash!

The gates loom. Hannah speeds towards them.

> *We're going to crash!*

> JIM
> *Just fucking do it!*

Hannah reaches and buckles her seat belt. Jim and Selena brace for impact . . .

They hit the gates, hard. Jim and Selena fly towards the perspex divider.

Freeze. Held. Fade to black.

Caption:

28 DAYS LATER

Fade up to:

EXT. FIELD. DAY.

A green field, with three white letters laid out across the grass. Spelling:

HELL

INT. FARMHOUSE — BEDROOM. DAY.

Waking from a nightmare, Jim's eyes snap open with a sharp intake of breath.

An echo of when we first saw him lying in hospital. But this time, when we pull away, we see he is lying on a double bed, in the bedroom of a small farmhouse.

Alone. But Selena's clothes are scattered.

Jim rises.

He looks around. Bright daylight is flooding into the room through the window.

JIM

Jesus. Not the curtains too.

INT. FARMHOUSE. DAY.

Jim walks down the stairs and peers into a living room – where he sees the sofa, with its covers removed.

INT. FARMHOUSE — KITCHEN. DAY.

Jim enters – to find Selena sat surrounded by lengths of material which she is stitching together.

He picks up a length of red material. Once part of the dress.

JIM
You looked all right in this, you know.

Selena ignores him.

Jim walks to the front door and opens it.

Pull back to reveal . . .

EXT. FARMHOUSE. DAY.

A stunning view.

A Lakeland valley, with a single farmhouse, and the black cab parked outside.

Also outside is Hannah, who is arranging huge lengths of material on the grass.

From our ground-level angle, there is no sense to be made of what Hannah is doing.

And we keep pulling back . . .

EXT. LAKELAND VALLEY. DAY.

. . . fast, down the valley, along a single ribbon of road.

Past a sign: Langdale Valley . . .

Further, now over a mile distant from the farmhouse, then:

Stopping, abruptly.

At a single Infected, who sits, emaciated, in the middle of the road.

A quiet moment with the starving, emaciated Infected. It is so weak it can hardly move. Only blink.

Then, in the background, a distant rush of noise, the low roar of a jet engine.

Slowly, the Infected turns its head upwards, where, in the clear blue sky, it sees:

A vapour trail.

A plane.

EXT. VALLEY. DAY.

A silent bird's eye view, looking down, at the valley floor and the farmhouse.

Where, outside, we now make sense of the stitched sheets and curtains, as they form letters on the grass below:

HELL

But tiny figures are forming a new letter. An O:

HELLO

Then, in the background, the sound of the jet, the rush of noise.

HANNAH
There! THERE!

Cut to:

Jim, Hannah and Selena look down the valley, where . . .

. . . screaming towards them, flying low along the valley floor, comes a jet plane.

They stand transfixed as the plane races towards them.

As it passes over, flying directly overhead, the terrific wash of air and noises whips around them, connected with a colossal sonic boom . . .

The boom rolls away, and the plane has passed . . .

Around Jim, Selena and Hannah, the sheets and material of the letters, ripped into the air, now spiral to the ground, falling around them.

JIM
Do you think he saw us this time?

Cut to black.

End.